At Issue

| Money Laundering

Other Books in the At Issue Series

At Issue

| Money Laundering

Lisa Idzikowski, Book Editor

GREENHAVEN
PUBLISHING

Published in 2021 by Greenhaven Publishing, LLC
353 3rd Avenue, Suite 255, New York, NY 10010

Articles in Greenhaven Publishing anthologies are often edited for length to meet page
requirements. In addition, original titles of these works are changed to clearly present
the main thesis and to explicitly indicate the author's opinion. Every effort is made to
ensure that Greenhaven Publishing accurately reflects the original intent of the authors.
Every effort has been made to trace the owners of the copyrighted material.

Cover image: Africa Studio/Shutterstock.com

Library of Congress Cataloging-in-Publication Data

Names: Idzikowski, Lisa, editor.
Title: Money laundering / Lisa Idzikowski, book editor.
Description: New York : Greenhaven Publishing, 2021. | Series: At issue |
   Includes bibliographical references and index. | Audience: Grades 9–12.
Identifiers: LCCN 2020005621 | ISBN 9781534507333 (library binding) | ISBN
   9781534507326 (paperback)
Subjects: LCSH: Money laundering—Juvenile literature. | Money—Law and
   legislation—Juvenile literature.
Classification: LCC HV8079.M64 M66 2020 | DDC 364.16/8—dc23
LC record available at https://lccn.loc.gov/2020005621

Manufactured in the United States of America

Website: http://greenhavenpublishing.com

Contents

Introduction

Many people are familiar with certain types of crime—armed robbery, human trafficking, drug smuggling, assault, terrorist bombings, and more. But what about money laundering? It falls under a broader category of crime known as white-collar crime. A simplified definition from *Merriam-Webster* states that an individual has "to transfer (illegally obtained money or investments) through an outside party to conceal the true source."[1] According to the United States Department of the Treasury:

> money laundering generally refers to financial transactions in which criminals, including terrorist organizations, attempt to disguise the proceeds, sources or nature of their illicit activities. Money laundering facilitates a broad range of serious underlying criminal offenses and ultimately threatens the integrity of the financial system.[2]

According to statistics from the FBI, violent crime in the US fell by 51 percent between 1993 and 2018.[3] Surprisingly, a 2016 survey found that 57 percent of registered US voters claimed they felt crime had gotten worse since 2008 despite this fact.[4] Money laundering may not be classified as a violent crime and may not be commonly recognized by many people, but it is an issue that has important consequences on international and domestic politics, the economy, and society as a whole.

Money laundering occurs around the world. The United Nations Office on Drugs and Crime estimates that as much as two trillion dollars are laundered annually,[5] and the International Monetary Fund and World Bank believe that criminals launder about two to four trillion dollars each year.[6] The US State Department published in its *2019 International Narcotics Control Strategy Report* a list of jurisdictions that are vulnerable to money laundering, which includes almost forty countries in the Americas and the Caribbean, over ten in Africa, over ten in Europe, nine in the former Soviet Union, three in the Middle East, and over ten in Asia.[7] Each of these countries are considered a "major money laundering country" and places where "financial institutions engage in currency transactions involving significant amount of proceeds from international narcotics trafficking."[8]

So how and why does money laundering take place? Simply put, money laundering is used by criminals. They need to somehow take illegally obtained money and transform it into seemingly legal tender so that they can spend it without raising suspicion. A well-known money laundering operation that took place from 2010 until 2014 called "The Laundromat" reportedly laundered $20 billion to $80 billion worth of dirty or illegal money.[9] This scheme involved multiple Russian banks and businesses, and the dirty money was filtered through fake companies—known as "shell companies"—in over ninety countries worldwide, including the US, UK, China, France, and Germany. Smaller countries like Taiwan and Slovenia also received funds. All in all, it was estimated that over $700 million went to the UK and over $60 million ended up in the US. A wide variety of goods and services were paid for using these illegal funds, including furs and diamonds, home cinema equipment, high priced private schools, aesthetic dentistry, expensive watches, and other items.

Not all money laundering is done in exactly the same manner, but according to the US Crimes and Financial Network, which is a bureau of the US Department of the Treasury, there is a general pattern to how it plays out:

> Typically, it involves three steps: placement, layering and integration. First, the illegitimate funds are furtively introduced into the legitimate financial system. Then, the money is moved around to create confusion, sometimes by wiring or transferring through numerous accounts. Finally, it is integrated into the financial system through additional transactions until the "dirty

money" appears "clean." Money laundering can facilitate crimes such as drug trafficking and terrorism and can adversely impact the global economy.[10]

Interestingly, advanced technologies often play an important role in money laundering schemes. Some make it easier for criminals to complete their illegal activities. Imagine you have $1 million in cash. That much money weighs about one hundred pounds, and specially trained detection dogs can notice its scent within seconds. Do you have dreams of owning fancy cars, big diamonds, designer clothes, or a big apartment? What if someone were to waltz into a car dealership or jewelry store and try to pay for something in cash amounting to $10,000 or more? According to the US Internal Revenue Service, any business or bank must report large cash transactions by filing a government form.[11] This is aimed at preventing money laundering.

Money launderers have found other ways to circumvent this issue through the use of technology. They have turned to alternate forms of payment such as stored-value cards—which are similar to gift cards—or cryptocurrencies. Law enforcement agencies know that criminals are using stored-value cards, but unlike the $10,000 rule there is no regulation concerning these cards. Cryptocurrencies such as Bitcoin are becoming the method of choice for money scammers. It is interesting to note that according to the Pew Research Center, about half of all Americans surveyed in 2016 had heard of Bitcoin—the original and most widely used cryptocurrency as of 2018—but relatively few actually used it. Just 1 percent of Americans had ever used, collected, or traded in Bitcoin.[12]

Experts in law enforcement, financial systems, and many other avenues of society know that money laundering involving cryptocurrencies is increasingly being used to support various illegal activities. Can anything be done to prevent it? Countries and governments around the world are attempting to make money laundering of any sort much more challenging. They also are trying to help businesses and financial entities more easily detect illegal activity. There is no doubt that leaders around the world recognize the hazards and negative consequences that money laundering poses, and they are putting great efforts into stemming this criminal enterprise. Whether or not the current and proposed strategies will work is another question. As has been demonstrated throughout history, criminals and criminal networks put great effort into staying ahead of the law and use almost any possible means to do so.

The topic of money laundering is a multifaceted issue that involves many aspects of society and commerce. As with any complex topic, experts from a wide range of fields have worthwhile ideas to share regarding how money laundering is used and how it may be possible to prevent it. As such, the viewpoints in *At Issue: Money Laundering* aim to shed light on this important issue through giving readers access to a range of perspectives.

Notes

1. "Launder," *Merriam-Webster*, https://www.merriam-webster.com/dictionary/launder.

2. "Money Laundering," US Department of the Treasury, https://home.treasury.gov/policy-issues/terrorism-and-illicit-finance/money-laundering.

3. John Gramlich, "5 facts about crime in the US," Pew Research Center, October 17, 2019, https://www.pewresearch.org/fact-tank/2019/10/17/facts-about-crime-in-the-u-s/.

4. *Ibid.*

5. Steven M. D'Antuono, "Combating Money Laundering and Other Forms of Illicit Finance: Regulator and Law Enforcement Perspectives on Reform," FBI, November 29, 2018, https://www.fbi.gov/news/testimony/combating-money-laundering-and-other-forms-of-illicit-finance.

6. Rhoda Weeks-Brown, "Cleaning Up," International Monetary Fund Finance and Development, December 2018, https://www.imf.org/external/pubs/ft/fandd/2018/12/imf-anti-money-laundering-and-economic-stability-straight.htm.

7. "2019 International Narcotics Control Strategy Report," US Department of State, March 28, 2019, https://www.state.gov/2019-international-narcotics-control-strategy-report/.

8. *Ibid.*

9. Luke Harding, "Deutsche Bank faces action over $20bn Russian money-laundering scheme," *Guardian*, April 17, 2019, https://www.theguardian.com/business/2019/apr/17/deutsche-bank-faces-action-over-20bn-russian-money-laundering-scheme.

10. "History of Anti-Money Laundering Laws," Financial Crimes Enforcement Network, https://www.fincen.gov/history-anti-money-laundering-laws.

11. "Cash payment report helps government combat money laundering," IRS, February 2019, https://www.irs.gov/newsroom/cash-payment-report-helps-government-combat-money-laundering.

12. Aaron Smith and Monica Anderson, "New modes of payment and the 'cashless economy'," Pew Research Center, December 19, 2016, https://www.pewresearch.org/internet/2016/12/19/new-modes-of-payment-and-the-cashless-economy/.

1

Money Laundering Explained

International Compliance Association

The International Compliance Association (ICA) is a professional organization for the global regulatory and financial crimes compliance community. ICA has offices around the world and includes over 150 member countries. The organization educates individuals interested in the prevention of financial crime and money laundering.

What exactly is money laundering? Is it always illegal, or are there legal applications? Money laundering is a process in which individuals try to make money obtained from illegal sources appear to be legal or legitimately obtained. There are many instances of illegal crimes and many—but not all—result in the need to launder money. This viewpoint explains the basics of money laundering and the processes involved in it, including the three primary stages of money laundering.

M oney laundering is the generic term used to describe the process by which criminals disguise the original ownership and control of the proceeds of criminal conduct by making such proceeds appear to have derived from a legitimate source.

The processes by which criminally derived property may be laundered are extensive. Though criminal money may be successfully laundered without the assistance of the financial sector,

"What is money laundering?" International Compliance Association. Reprinted by permission.

the reality is that hundreds of billions of dollars of criminally derived money is laundered through financial institutions, annually. The nature of the services and products offered by the financial services industry (namely managing, controlling and possessing money and property belonging to others) means that it is vulnerable to abuse by money launderers.

How Is the Offence of Money Laundering Committed?

Money laundering offences have similar characteristics globally. There are two key elements to a money laundering offence:

1. The necessary act of laundering itself i.e. the provision of financial services; and
2. A requisite degree of knowledge or suspicion (either subjective or objective) relating to the source of the funds or the conduct of a client.

The act of laundering is committed in circumstances where a person is engaged in an arrangement (i.e. by providing a service or product) and that arrangement involves the proceeds of crime. These arrangements include a wide variety of business relationships e.g. banking, fiduciary and investment management.

The requisite degree of knowledge or suspicion will depend upon the specific offence but will usually be present where the person providing the arrangement, service or product knows, suspects or has reasonable grounds to suspect that the property involved in the arrangement represents the proceeds of crime. In some cases the offence may also be committed where a person knows or suspects that the person with whom he or she is dealing is engaged in or has benefited from criminal conduct.

Are All Crimes Capable of Predicating Money Laundering?

Different jurisdictions define crime predicating the offence of money laundering in different ways. Generally the differences between the definitions may be summarised as follows:

1. Differences in the degree of severity of crime regarded as sufficient to predicate an offence of money laundering. For example in some jurisdictions it is defined as being any crime that would be punishable by one or more years imprisonment. In other jurisdictions the necessary punishment may be three or five years imprisonment; or

2. Differences in the requirement for the crime to be recognized both in the country where it took place and by the laws of the jurisdiction where the laundering activity takes place or simply a requirement for the conduct to be regarded as a crime in the country where the laundering activity takes place irrespective of how that conduct is treated in the country where it took place.

In practice almost all serious crimes, including, drug trafficking, terrorism, fraud, robbery, prostitution, illegal gambling, arms trafficking, bribery and corruption are capable of predicating money laundering offences in most jurisdictions.

Can Fiscal Offences Such As Tax Evasion Predicate Money Laundering?

The answer depends upon the definition of crime contained within the money laundering legislation of a particular jurisdiction.

Tax evasion and other fiscal offences are treated as predicate money laundering crimes in most of the worlds most effectively regulated jurisdictions.

Why Is Money Laundering Illegal?

The objective of the criminalisation of money laundering is to take the profit out of crime. The rationale for the creation of the offence is that it is wrong for individuals and organisations to assist criminals to benefit from the proceeds of their criminal activity or to facilitate the commission of such crimes by providing financial services to them.

How Is Money Laundered?

The processes are extensive. Generally speaking, money is laundered whenever a person or business deals in any way with another person's benefit from crime. That can occur in a countless number of diverse ways.

Traditionally money laundering has been described as a process which takes place in three distinct stages.

- **Placement**, the stage at which criminally derived funds are introduced in the financial system.
- **Layering**, the substantive stage of the process in which the property is 'washed' and its ownership and source is disguised.
- **Integration**, the final stage at which the 'laundered' property is re-introduced into the legitimate economy.

This three staged definition of money laundering is highly simplistic. The reality is that the so called stages often overlap and in some cases, for example in cases of financial crimes, there is no requirement for the proceeds of crime to be "placed."

2

How Banks Facilitate International Money Laundering Schemes

Luke Harding

Luke Harding is a foreign correspondent for the Guardian *who has reported from Moscow, Delhi, and Berlin. He has covered the wars in Libya, Afghanistan, and Iraq. He is the author of* Collusion: How Russia Helped Trump Win the White House.

Money laundering occurs in many countries around the globe. One of Germany's largest banks—Deutsche Bank—was caught in a scheme tied to criminals in Russia that took place between 2010 and 2014 and involved laundering $20 billion. The scheme has likely affected many businesses and institutions in the United States, United Kingdom, various European countries, and—according to some sources—possibly even US president Donald Trump. The Deutsche Bank is now attempting to increase its anti-financial crime response.

Germany's troubled Deutsche Bank faces fines, legal action and the possible prosecution of "senior management" because of its role in a $20bn Russian money-laundering scheme, a confidential internal report seen by the Guardian says.

The bank admits there is a high risk that regulators in the US and UK will take "significant disciplinary action" against it. Deutsche concedes that the scandal has hurt its "global brand"—

"Deutsche Bank faces action over $20bn Russian money-laundering scheme," by Luke Harding, Guardian News and Media Limited, April 17, 2019. Reprinted by permission.

and is likely to cause "client attrition," loss of investor confidence and a decline in its market value.

Deutsche Bank was embroiled in a vast money-laundering operation, dubbed the Global Laundromat. Russian criminals with links to the Kremlin, the old KGB and its main successor, the FSB, used the scheme between 2010 and 2014 to move money into the western financial system. The cash involved could total $80bn, detectives believe.

Shell companies typically based in the UK "loaned" money to each other. Companies then defaulted on this large fictitious debt. Corrupt judges in Moldova authenticated the debt—with billions transferred to Moldova and the Baltics via a bank in Latvia.

Deutsche Bank was used to launder the money via its corresponding banking network—effectively allowing illegal Russian payments to be funnelled to the US, the European Union and Asia.

The bank was entirely unaware of the scam until the Guardian and Organised Crime and Corruption Reporting Project (OCCRP) broke the story in March 2017, the report says. The first it knew was an email from the Guardian and Germany's Süddeutsche Zeitung newspaper asking for comment.

"Only with this intelligence received is it now possible for Deutsche Bank to start global investigations," it notes.

In the embarrassing aftermath, the bank asked two in-house financial crime investigators—Philippe Vollot and Hinrich Völcker—to find out what had gone wrong. Their nine-page presentation was shared last year with the audit committee of the bank's supervisory board and is marked "strictly confidential."

The pair identified numerous "high-risk entities." They included 1,244 in the US, 329 in the UK and 950 in Germany. These entities were responsible for nearly 700,000 transactions, the report says, involving at least £62m in the UK, $47m in the US, and €55m in Germany.

As part of its investigation, Deutsche Bank sent 149 "suspicious activity reports" to the National Crime Agency in London. Similar disclosures of potential money-laundering transactions were made to authorities in the US and elsewhere—with 30 private and corporate Deutsche Bank clients reported. Some may have been "unknowingly used," the report says.

The affair is a further blow to Deutsche Banks's ailing reputation. It comes amid police raids on its Frankfurt HQ over the Panama Papers, a plunging share price and talks over a possible merger with Germany's Commerzbank. The raid last November came after German prosecutors alleged two bank employees helped clients launder money via offshore firms.

Deutsche is also under scrutiny in Washington over its financial dealings with Donald Trump. On 15 April, Democrats from the House intelligence and financial services committees issued a subpoena, demanding the bank provide documents about its lending to the president.

Over two decades, Trump borrowed more than $2bn from Deutsche. In 2008, he defaulted on a $45m loan repayment and sued the bank. Its private wealth division in New York subsequently loaned Trump a further $300m—a move that bemused insiders and which has yet to be fully explained.

In recent years, the bank has had a series of bruising encounters with international regulators. Between 2011 and 2018, it paid $14.5bn in fines, with exposure to dubious Russian money a regular theme.

In 2017, the UK's Financial Conduct Authority imposed its largest fine—£163m—after Deutsche carried out a $10bn "mirror trade" scheme run out of its branch in Moscow. The New York Department of Financial Services (DFS) fined the bank $425m over the same case, in which roubles were converted into dollars via fake trades on behalf of VIP Russian clients.

Deutsche carried out an internal investigation into the "mirror trades" affair, "Project Square." The leaked Global Laundromat report says there is "no systematic link" between the two Russian money-laundering schemes. However, it suggests some overlap.

Two unnamed entities feature in both and 46 "mirror trade" entities "directly transacted" with 233 laundromat ones.

The leaked report says Deutsche has cleaned up its act. It says it has stopped doing business with the two banks at the centre of the Laundromat scandal—Moldova's Moldindconbank and Latvia's Trasta Komercbanka. Regulators in Latvia closed down Trasta in 2016 because of serial money-laundering violations.

Deutsche Bank says it has "reduced its footprint" across the post-Soviet region. It no longer has relationships with any banks in Moldova, Latvia, Estonia and Cyprus, the report says. All are favourite destinations for illicit Moscow money. The bank has scaled down its business activities in Russia and Ukraine, it says.

The bank is under investigation for its role in Europe's biggest banking scandal, involving Denmark's Danske Bank. Danske laundered €200bn (£178bn) of Russian money via its branch in Estonia. Deutsche provided correspondent banking services via its US subsidiary.

Deutsche Bank said it could not comment on "potential or ongoing investigations," or on "any matters regarding our regulators." It said it was committed to providing "appropriate information to all authorised Investigations."

The bank said: "We have considerably increased staff numbers in anti-financial crime and more than tripled our staff since 2015. Since 2016 we have invested €700m in upgrading our key control functions there."

3

Money Laundering Is Common in Iran

Ken Maginnis

Major Kenneth Maginnis is a politician from Northern Ireland and a member of the House of Lords in the UK Parliament.

Money laundering is very common in Iran, and according to some Iran is the top place for money laundering in the world. It is such a common phenomenon that even politicians and other officials in the country admit that it is occurring everywhere in Iran. Many people are benefitting from these long-accepted activities, and although some influential people in the country want to enact laws to prevent illegal activities, they are coming up against many obstacles.

It was reported that the Expediency Council has approved a bill paving the way for Iran to join the FATF, but Gholamreza Mesbahi Moghaddam, a member of the council, was quoted by Fars News Agency saying "The bill approved by the council was an amendment to the internal mechanism set up for countering money laundering and contrary to what has been quoted by some media is has no connection with the Islamic Republic to FATF."

Corruption through money laundering is rampant in Iran. Among some indexes, Iran ranks 1st in the world in money laundering, ahead of Afghanistan and Tajikistan.

In a recent interview with state television, Mohammad Javad Zarif admitted, "Money laundering is a fact in our country."

"Money Laundering in Iran is Pervasive," by Ken Maginnis, International Policy Digest, January 7, 2019. Reprinted by permission.

He added: "I know people who, for example, earned a profit of 30 trillion tomans ($7 billion) in a transfer deal."

This is not a new phenomenon. On March 2016, Rahmani Fazli, Iran's interior minister, said: "Undoubtedly part of the dirty money of drug trafficking will enter politics, elections and the transfer of political power in the country."

Of course, it is not clear exactly how much money is laundered in Iran, but statistics suggest that it is astronomical.

Pedram Soltani, vice president of the Chamber of Commerce, confirms the regime's estimate at $35 billion, while other sources put the number closer to $42 billion.

"The money from organized crime or drug trafficking is now an integral element within the banking system and we do not know the source and destination of money from organized crimes," said Jonaidi, legal advisor to President Rouhani.

Besides money, the smuggling of goods is also problematic for the regime. At least 40% of the goods are imported into Iran by smugglers.

Failure to return dollars earned from exports is part of the process of money laundering in Iran. "Since the beginning of the year, we had $27 billion worth of non-oil exports, but less than $7 billion is back to the system, and I don't know where the rest of it is," said Amir Hemmati, the head of Iran's Central Bank, in an interview with state television in November.

The obvious question now is who is the biggest culprit? It is undoubtedly the Revolutionary Guards Corps (IRGC). "We have documented statistics; many exporters took the dollar at 5-6 thousand tomans. There are a total of 250 exporters who have not yet brought back their currencies to the economic cycle since the beginning of this year."

While neither Hemmati nor Zarif, specifically identified those who "benefit from money laundering," the reaction of some members of parliament made it clear that Zarif was referring to the Revolutionary Guards Corps. Zolnour, a former IRGC commander, responded immediately to Zarif's interview and demanded that he produce evidence for his claims.

Another member of parliament affiliated with the IRGC also demanded clarification from Zarif. "If Zarif does not prove money laundering, the prosecutor has the right to prosecute him," said MP Karimi Ghoddoosi.

Morteza Saffari-Natanzai, another MP, said: "Money laundering is an economic issue related to internal affairs, and is not in the field of foreign policy that the Minister has commented on."

Within the regime, disputes are intensifying to adopt laws that would bring Iran into compliance with the anti-money laundering standards of the French-headquartered Financial Action Task Force (FATC). In early December, President Rouhani suggested that the IRGC's continued opposition to such laws would cost the Iranian economy.

But the IRGC says that if Iran cooperates with the FATF, its money laundering networks will be identified and placed on the sanctions list, meaning it's better to pay the cost of money laundering than to risk increased international isolation.

Money-laundering activities of IRGC are not only limited to Iran. Recently, a judicial investigation was launched to identify the IRGC money laundering network in Bahrain. The network is accused of money laundering with drug trafficking networks. The network operated in some parts of the region by secretly selling drugs abroad.

4

Ethiopia Has Problems with Money Laundering Because of Illicit Cash

Ashenafi Endale

Ashenafi Endale is a writer for the Ethiopian Business Review.

Ethiopia, like many developing countries, faces various obstacles in its financial systems. One of the biggest issues is that the banking system is underdeveloped and consequently people rely on cash for everyday monetary transactions. The usual criminal enterprises of drug and human trafficking, terrorism, and weapons smuggling contribute to Ethiopia's problems, but other areas that could be overlooked are also contributors. These areas include corruption, bribery, and forcing kickbacks. Ethiopia is making attempts to get these problems under control.

Nowadays, it is common to hear news stories about the arrest of people trying to leave the country with money, especially hard currency, via borders and airports. A couple of months ago, law enforcement even forced a plane to return to Addis Ababa's Bole International Airport hours after it took off, in order to arrest a woman who had boarded the flight with close to half a million dollars in illegally smuggled money.

In line with the increasing illegal cross-border movement of capital, the number of cases filed in courts has also been mounting. Since 2014/15, close to 300 cases related to the illegal cross-border

"The Mounting Illicit Capital Out Flows From Ethiopia," by Ashenafi Endale, Ethiopian Business Review, January 16 - February 15, 2019. Reprinted by permission.

movement of capital were filed at the Lideta Federal High Court. 110 of those defendants have already been sentenced, and 99 of the cases are currently being heard. Each case involves sums of ETB50 to ETB300 million.

However, government officials stress that these cases are a very tiny portion of the illegal activity going on in the country. "It is like grabbing the tail of the devil," says Temesgen Lapiso, director of the Trans-Boundary Crimes Directorate at Lideta Federal High Court.

Indeed, in Ethiopia, illicit financial flow (IFF) is one of the most serious issues being faced by the government and law enforcement. According to the study released by Transparency International in September 2018, called "Illicit Financial Flows in Ethiopia" which covers the years 2005 to 2014, an estimated average of USD1.3 billion to USD3.2 billion has left Ethiopia in the form of IFFs every year. The annual capital flow from Ethiopia is equivalent to about 11Pct to 29Pct of the country's total trade, 40Pct to 97Pct of aid, or 10Pct to 30Pct of the government's annual revenue.

Roots of IFFs

Although there is no single agreed on definition of IFF among scholars, the concept is related to the laundering of illegal capital from a country's proceeds of crime, corruption and tax evasion. There could be different causes of capital flight, ranging from political reasons like regime changes, to a decline in economic stability and strict capital regulations. Sakshi Rai, Programme Consultant at the Centre for Budget and Governance Accountability, a think-tank focusing on public policies and government finance in India, in a 2017 study titled "The Specter of Illicit Financial Flows," classified these factors in to four groups: informal sector, crime, trade, and tax related.

One of the informal sector related factors that pushes capital out from most developing, low income countries like Ethiopia, is the absence of proper banking systems and institutions as well as the dominance of cash based transactions, which creates informal or underground banking channels. "Ethiopia is highly exposed to illicit capital flow mainly due to its dominant cash based economy," argues Paschal Anosike (PhD), director of the Centre for African Entrepreneurship and Leadership at the University of Wolverhampton. "Cash is in the hands of people beyond the banking system. Therefore it is difficult to trace money, abnormal transactions and currencies."

Rai points out when the official banking system is weak, people tend to rely on personal relationships, bonds and networks to transfer funds. These funds, in turn, can be used by criminals and the general public to move large sums of money across borders. As the experience of many countries all over the world shows, informal money laundering channels include a traditional system of transferring money commonly known as hawala, which is used mostly by African and Arab countries, as well as the hundi network that is the dominant method of fund transfer in South Asia.

Tesfaye Gebreegziabher (Commander), acting director of the Financial Transactions Examinations and Analysis Directorate at the Finance Intelligence Center (FIC), agrees with the notion that the informal remittance systems in Ethiopia are the main sources of IFFs. "The money obtained from informal operators in the black market from the Diaspora community who want to send money to their families in Ethiopia is used to pay off corrupt officials or to reduce the risk of being charged," he argues. "The money is also used to acquire properties in other countries by a growing number of business and political elites."

Stakeholders stress that a shortage of hard currency is the primary reason for the thriving informal fund channels, which in turn, facilitates illicit capital flows. As a result, Ethiopians who run businesses, usually restaurants and shops, as well as unauthorized agents, collect the hard currency from the Diaspora. The official revenue from remittances is currently USD3.5 billion. "The loss due to illegal remittances is at least twice the official figure," says Temesgen. "Informal remittance channels are damaging the economy by facilitating the transfer of capital out of the country."

However, a bank manager, who asked to remain anonymous, argues that it is wrong to conclude that the fundamental reason for the existence of informal fund transfer channels is the hard currency shortage. "I believe illicit trades continue even if there is surplus hard currency because the informal economy always rewards with more profit," he said.

In addition to remittances, the other source of hard currency is Ethiopian exporters. "They report lower exports than the actual volume and earn less foreign currency through official channels while keeping the difference in offshore accounts, where it is availed for anybody who wants to use it," adds Gashaw Tamiru, director of Corporate Law and Human Right Directorate at Lideta Federal High Court.

Addisu Habba, president of Debub Global Bank, however, argues it is all about the mismatch between demand and supply. "Since the Dergue regime, Ethiopia has never had enough foreign exchange to cover its import bills. The main task should be increasing the supply of foreign currency."

Yet, because owners of illicitly obtained finance are more interested in hiding their money than maximizing its return, Rai argues that macroeconomic factors have little impact when it comes to capital flight. Rather, it is crime related activities including corruption that influence illicit financial flow in a significant manner.

Gashaw says Ethiopia loses a significant portion of revenue due to crime related activities along border areas. "In addition, the overall foreign trade is sabotaged by corrupt officials and illicit traders. Many commodities, including money, are traded illegally. The illicit finance flow," Gashaw argues, "is higher than we know, if all of the commodities are included in the calculation.'

Although drug and human trafficking, terrorism and illegal weapons trades all contribute to capital flight, corruption is one of the major catalysts for illicit finance in Ethiopia. In fact, a significant amount of money is lost to corruption, rent-seeking practices, kickbacks, and bribery. According to Transparency

International, Ethiopia ranked 107 out of 176 countries in the Corruption Perception Index last year.

According to the United Nations Development Programme, weak governance generates public corruption and promotes corporate malfeasance. These, in turn, make sending capital out of the country easy. The role of a fragile government in exacerbating illicit capital outflows is also supported by studies that prove the existence of strong correlation between debt accumulation by developing countries and illicit financial flows.

However, the major cause of illicit capital flight in Ethiopia, accounting for 55Pct to 80Pct of the total value, is trade related, and in particular, capital flight through trade mis-invoicing. Abdulmenan Mohammed Hamza, a financial expert with over 20 years of experience, says a large portion of illicit capital flow in Ethiopia is related to foreign trade. "Illegal profit transfer is a common feature of illicit financial flow in Ethiopia," he told EBR.

Trade mis-invoicing is defined as misstating the value, quantity, or composition of goods on customs declaration forms and invoices, mainly for the purposes of money laundering and tax evading. Studies conducted on the subject reveal that trade mis invoicing can occur in to three ways: import over invoicing, export under-invoicing and export over-invoicing.

Import over-invoicing disguises the movement of capital out of a country by using false agreements that indicate a price higher than the original in order to get hard currency from local commercial banks. "Commercial banks ask importers to present agreements between them and foreign suppliers in order to start the process of granting foreign currency," explains Abdulmenan. "But the banks' efforts to validate the creditability of the price are inadequate."

Of course, insiders stress that the lack of a national price index or a directive that allows banks to crosscheck the validity of the prices in the agreement worsens the problem. "Banks often don't record hard currency requests on official bank sheets. Instead, they have separate records," argues Temesgen. "We have encountered various cases of this. All banks have such systems, down to their branches."

On the other hand, under-invoicing is a common practice by exporters in Ethiopia. Exporters negotiate with their business partners abroad and under-invoice their trade agreements. When payment is settled, exporters receive the under-invoiced price through local banks, while the rest is deposited in their foreign account.

However, the main motivation behind trade mis-invoicing is mainly tax evasion. For instance, importers can over invoice their prices in order to inflate their overall costs, which would lower the amount of taxes they owe the government. Exporters also under invoice contracts by lowering the volume of their shipment in order to evade or avoid taxes on corporate profits.

While tax evasion is clearly illegal, tax avoidance takes place through gaps in the laws, lapses in regulations and through unclear structures and arrangements, according to Rai. For instance, Ethiopia losses up to ETB60 billion tax revenue annually due to abuse of tax incentives, according to Adanach Abebe, minister of Revenues.

Ramifications

Although it is hidden by nature and estimates are uncertain, the consequences of IFF are immense. Rai stresses that a dollar lost due to illicit financial flow has more than one dollar's damage for a given country. For instance, if an exporter mis-invoices a trade agreement for the purpose of evading taxes, the loss to the public purse is not only the tax evaded, but possibly stolen treasury funds that are transferred through the same channels. In addition, the illicit capital that exits the country can be used to finance corruption and regenerate crime.

On the other hand, the study by Transparency International reveals that capital departed from Ethiopia has led to an economic loss of 2.2 percentage points on average, annually. It also estimated that had it not been for IFFs, poverty would have been reduced by about 2.5 percentage points in the last ten years.

Taming the Problem

Many of the actions taken by the government, such as taking suspected offenders to court, have not been successful. "We have run many operations and forwarded hundreds of cases to the police. But almost all of them were dropped through the court processes. Therefore, we stopped taking cases to court last year. But we started again last month," explains Tesfaye. "Even if black market operators are caught and sentenced, their hard currency and other assets are never confiscated by the government. Even if it is, it never goes to the government's coffers."

The FIC conducted a study to identify the sources of illicit capital flight five years ago. But Tesfaye says the problem could not be solved because of an inefficient court system and high corruption. "Law enforcement agencies are weak in collecting evidence. The Federal Police Commission has limited capacity and expertise to investigate."

On top of these, the establishment proclamation of the FIC does not give it the power to investigate and prosecute these crimes. "Plus, The FIC usually lacks budget. The Financial Transactions Examinations and Analysis Directorate at FIC only have nine employees, despite it needing at least 50. The same directorate in South Africa has 300 employees," adds Tesfaye.

Mignot Denekew, attorney of organized and border crossing crimes at Lideta Federal High Court, agrees that very limited efforts have been made to bring economic crimes to court. "Even if cases come to court, it is difficult to convince the court that illicit finance is hurting the country. This is because most of the illicit finance activities and underground economy transaction systems seem technically legal."

Indeed, there is an ongoing debate about the definition of IFFs and the need for widening it beyond "dirty money" to include financial flows associated with tax avoidance, which, in many cases can be legal. In fact, Rai indicates that there are circumstances in which trade mis-invoicing has been confused with price transfer or profit repatriation, which are legal practices, especially among multinational companies.

Although the country introduced the Prevention and Suppression of Money Laundering and Financing Terrorism Proclamation in 2013, according to a study conducted by Transparency International, its focus is restricted to controlling financing terrorism and money laundering while giving little emphasis to illicit capital outflows from Ethiopia. This is why stakeholders stress that Ethiopia needs to adopt and enforce policies that promote good governance, tackle corruption, go after dirty money and implement transparent tax systems to reverse the situation.

5

Terrorists Finance Their Operations Using Shell Companies

Shima Baradaran Baughman

Shima Baradaran Baughman is a law professor at the University of Utah. Her research focuses on criminal procedure, criminal law, and international law. She is an expert on the issues of bail and pretrial prediction.

Money laundering and tax evasion are bad enough, but what about when they're used to finance terrorism? Leaked documents demonstrate how easy it is to form what is known as a "shell company" and then to use this entity to avoid paying taxes to one's country (if a person is rich) or to finance global terrorism. Terrorists need lots of money to finance their insidious operations, so it is logical to assume that the ease and availability of shell company formation must be stopped to help fight against it.

The Panama Papers have exposed the largest financial crime scandal of our lifetimes. But what has been uncovered by the Panama Papers is much more dangerous than simply greed and corruption.

For those of you who have been hiding under a rock, the Panama Papers are over 11 million documents leaked from Mossack Fonseca, one of the largest law firms in the world specializing in offshore accounts and incorporation of shell companies. According to these papers, some of which I reviewed personally as a legal collaborator with Fusion Media, over 200,000 international shell companies were formed for over 14,000 clients. Among these were over 140 politicians and their families and over a dozen political leaders and celebrities, including soccer star Lionel Messi.

The common link among these individuals is that they used shell companies and offshore accounts to shield their wealth from their home governments.

The media, politicians and the public are trying to make sense of what the Panama Papers means for (a lack of) regulation. There is grave concern about fairness, international tax schemes and shell companies. A particular focus of the current investigation is the widespread use (and abuse) of anonymous shell companies.

Shell companies are "hollow," meaning that they have no significant assets and may only be identifiable by a name and mailing address. Shell companies can be set up to hide assets from prying eyes. While they have a number of legitimate uses—such as mergers, holding assets during complex transactions and protecting trade secrets—anonymous shell companies are often used for tax evasion, fraud, money laundering and even to fund terrorism.

Oddly missing from the Panama Papers are American individuals. Why is it that high net worth individuals from around the world went to Panama to hide their money and none of them are Americans?

One reason is that the US has a lower tax burden than Europe for the high net worth individual.

But the biggest reason is that an American has no need to form a shell company in Panama because they can obtain one right here in the United States. And as my research shows, it's incredibly easy to do. Unfortunately, that's something terrorist organizations can take advantage of as well.

How to Make a Shell Company for Your Cat

The fact is that shell companies are as easy to form in the US as they are in Panama.

Panama has very few regulations on the formation of shell companies. But neither does the United States. Nearly two million corporations and limited liability companies are formed every year in the United States, and most jurisdictions do not require any identity documentation whatsoever.

In fact, Fusion—one of the media companies that had access to Fonseca documents—demonstrated on video that one of its collaborators was able to form a Delaware shell company for her cat. This took only a few minutes, US$249 (via credit card) and required no identification documents at all.

Similarly lax regulations exist in Montana, Nevada and Wyoming. These states compete for clients, so there has been a race to the bottom in states wanting to require even less than the others in order to form a shell corporation.

With the ease of incorporation, some may choose to form companies for their pets. Others may decide to create companies to hide assets in for tax evasion or money laundering purposes. However, even more alarming is that terrorists can easily disguise their true identities from law enforcement through shell companies.

A potential terrorist cannot take a flight to neighboring states without a passport or driver's license, but they can form a shell company without any information in a matter of minutes.

In a high-profile instance of this, for many years Russian arms dealer Viktor Bout used shell corporations to anonymously supply terrorist groups around the globe with major weaponry like tanks and shoulder-file missiles.

Terrorism and Offshore Financing

The life-blood of an effective terrorist network is financing. And shell companies facilitate the easy distribution of money.

ISIS makes $1 million to $2 million a day in oil production, has obtained over $100 million in ransoms from kidnapping and collects "taxes" from the 6 million people it has gained control over.

And al-Qaida's worldwide operations require $30-50 million per year. The September 11 attacks, for example, cost approximately $500,000.

But not every terrorist attack requires large sums of money. The London transit bombings cost a mere $15,000 and the Paris bombings cost about $10,000 or less. Funding a terrorism enterprise is easily done under the cover of shell companies.

In contrast, the United States has spent (as of 2014) over $1.6 trillion since September 11, 2001 on its major military operations abroad and $9 million a day just on fighting ISIS.

If we want to fight terrorism effectively, we should also be cracking down on terrorism financing. Given the ease and persistence of terrorist financing—particularly using shell companies—a shift in attention on financial regulations that would stop terrorism financing would be a good start.

International regulations do exist to limit the formation of shell companies without a passport or drivers license. The United States and over 180 countries have actually enacted a series of identity reporting requirements. Organizations such as the Financial Action Task Force, the World Bank, the UN and the EU have also taken steps to "blacklist" countries that do not comply. The United States has implemented a host of measures, including the use of "terrorist designations" and Suspicious Activity Reports (SARs), to root out and eliminate risks in our financial institutions.

However, none of these regulations have been enacted by Congress, and so they are not binding to US states.

And no one has studied how effective these international standards are on limiting financial crime. Until recently.

A Shell Game

My coauthors, Mike Findley, Dan Nielson, Jason Sharman and I conducted a study in University of Pennsylvania Law Review to answer two central questions: first, how easy is it to form an anonymous shell company and, second, how effective are international and domestic regulations at curbing their illegitimate uses.

In the course of our study, we sent emails to thousands of firms around the world and asked for their assistance in forming an anonymous shell company. In some, we posed as low-risk businesses looking for guidance, in others, we posed as terrorists or offered premiums for secrecy. The results were startling.

Most surprising was the fact that some firms were more likely to offer their assistance when we posed as terrorists than when we posed as businesses from wealthy, industrialized nations such as the United States.

Countries like the British Virgin Islands, Cayman Islands and Isle of Man—though widely considered "tax havens"—were among the most compliant countries in the world. That is, they followed international rules and made it difficult to set up shell companies without following proper procedures.

The United States, however, ranked near the bottom. As did—unsurprisingly—Panama. It was easier to form a shell company in the United States than in any other country besides Kenya. Some of the worst offending states were also Delaware, Wyoming and Nevada, though compliance varied greatly as a number of states like Rhode Island and Utah had near-perfect compliance.

Getting Serious About Terrorist Financing

These results demonstrate that we are far from safe from the dangers of tax evasion, money laundering and even terrorist financing. And, in particular, the United States is a key international player in competing to form shell companies for the shadiest of actors.

Indeed, I would argue we have fallen well short of the mark on one of the most important goals in the war on terror: eliminating the network of terrorist financing.

It is clear that current regulations are not particularly effective, as firms are more willing than ever to aid in forming anonymous shell companies.

In order to be effective, countries must get serious about requiring identity documentation when businesses or individuals wish to form shell companies. Senator Carl Levin, for example, has for a number of years worked to pass the Incorporation Transparency and Law Enforcement Assistance Act, but to no avail.

More effective regulations are only a beginning. To be the most successful, the government will have to work with the financial sector to root out these lines of terrorist financing by enacting implementing regulations within the US that require identifying documents when forming a shell company. Many European countries and even the tax havens have enacted these laws, and it is time for the US to do the same.

As noted above, there are many legitimate business purposes for forming shell companies, so they should not be eliminated altogether. But we must become better at identifying clients, accounts and transactions that pose the greatest risk of international crime.

If the Panama Papers serve any purpose, it should be as a lesson to the world that there are worse things that can happen with shell companies than hiding money.

6

How Japan Fights Money Laundering in Cryptocurrency Exchange

Takero Minami

Takero Minami is a staff writer for the Nikkei Asian Review.

The cryptocurrency Bitcoin has been around for about ten years, and during that timespan many other cryptocurrencies have also been developed. This is not good news for those trying to crack down on money laundering. Japan is trying to do just that and has found the task to be challenging. Cryptocurrencies may be convenient for making purchases—especially between different countries—but for the same reasons they also make it easier for criminals to launder money. Japan has suffered from several recent large cryptocurrency thefts, and consequently it is upping its game regarding cryptocurrency regulation.

Last year authorities arrived at cryptocurrency exchange operator FSHO's one-room office in a Yokohama business district for an on-site inspection. They discovered multiple suspicious transactions.

The company had overlooked numerous transactions over a short period of time in which the same client converted large amounts of digital currency to cash, a person familiar with the investigation said. Japan's financial regulator, fearing that the funds

"Japan eyes cryptocurrencies as it toughens money laundering laws," by Takero Minami, Nikkei Inc., May 22, 2019, https://asia.nikkei.com/Spotlight/Bitcoin-evolution/Japan-eyes-cryptocurrencies-as-it-toughens-money-laundering-laws. Reprinted by permission.

had found their way to illicit actors, later declined the operator's bid to become a registered exchange, the first such rejection.

The Financial Services Agency is stepping up its countermeasures for money laundering, and that includes taking a hard look at cryptocurrency exchanges. Japan's anti-money laundering regime will undergo an inspection by an intergovernmental body this fall, and the FSA is eager for a good review.

The issue is also expected to be taken up at the G-20 meeting this summer. As the chair of this year's gathering, Japan does not want to fall behind other countries in implementing policies.

To ensure the country's financial security framework is in working order, the FSA is taking aim at cryptocurrency exchanges that do not adequately confirm their clients' identities or offer anonymous transactions, as well as at banks and other traditional financial institutions.

It has been 10 years since the birth of bitcoin, and during that time the digital currency's value has fluctuated wildly. Security remains an issue. Last May hackers stole $41 million worth of bitcoin from Binance, one of the world's largest cryptocurrency exchanges.

Now there are more than 2,000 cryptocurrencies. They have drawn acclaim as a next generation payments solution, thanks to the conveniences they offer, like remitting money across national borders without going through banks. But that ease of use means they can be used for illegal transactions and money laundering.

A panel of experts in March reported to the U.N. Security Council that North Korea used cyberattacks and blockchain technology to steal digital currency. They estimated that North Korea has successfully attacked Asian cryptocurrency exchanges at least five times, acquiring $571 million.

"Cyberattacks involving cryptocurrencies provide the Democratic People's Republic of Korea with more ways to evade sanctions given that they are harder to trace, can be laundered many times and are independent from government regulation," the panel wrote.

In April 2017, Japan became the first to introduce a registration system for cryptocurrency exchanges. Until then, there were no real rules governing exchange operators, but the government started putting regulations in place to combat money laundering.

Such countermeasures are a topic of global discussion. They are now under the purview of the Financial Action Task Force, a product of the 1989 G-7 summit. The intergovernmental FATF has a strong influence on the development of regulations and practical implementation of money laundering measures.

In October, its rules were changed such that money laundering regulations could also be applied to cryptocurrency exchanges. The change also called on member countries to develop licensing and registration systems, and to put in place measures that allow for monitoring.

The FATF's investigatory body will come to Japan this fall to assess domestic money laundering laws. It is expected to look at cryptocurrency exchange operators, banks and credit unions, according to a senior FSA official, so there is a pressing need to develop countermeasures.

Exchange companies are being asked to clearly explain what steps they are taking to prevent money laundering.

In Japan, exchanges came under the microscope after the theft of about 58 billion yen worth of cryptocurrency from Coincheck in January 2018. In June of that year the FSA took the unusual step of issuing business improvement orders to six other operators, citing insufficient money laundering countermeasures and other practices. In some cases, identity verification was insufficient, and clients were allowed to register post office boxes as personal addresses.

Japan has, at times, struggled to deal with money laundering. In its 2008 report, the FATF gave Japan its lowest possible rating in regard to financial institutions identifying their clients. In its statement, the group singled out Japan as having an insufficient legal framework.

For the FSA, the inspection this fall is a chance to expunge that blemish. "One company's problem can't help but affect the whole country's evaluation," said an official. "We'll continue with the on-site inspections, and we'll make sure everything is sound."

Ahead of the inspection, the G-20 next month is expected to discuss international regulations for cryptocurrencies. Japan will chair the G-20 summit in Osaka. The topic of initial coin offerings, a form of fundraising using digital currencies, could come up. While China and South Korea have banned ICOs, Japan continues to regulate the schemes.

Already, cryptocurrency exchanges are relocating to countries with looser regulations, like the Mediterranean country of Malta.

As the global cryptocurrency playing field shifts, the need for international coordination will only grow.

7

Criminals Use Large Banks Around the World to Launder Money

Jamie Redman

Jamie Redman is a financial tech journalist who has been an active member of the cryptocurrency community since 2011. He has written for Bitcoin.com *and is particularly knowledgeable about Bitcoin, open source code, and decentralized applications.*

Do you think that only criminals launder money? As it happens, this is not the case. Some of the world's largest banks and banking chains have been caught overlooking individuals and groups—including both criminals and politicians—laundering large amounts of money. There are several common ways that money is laundered using banks and banking accounts. Furthermore, banks are not the only businesses responsible for this criminal activity: real estate is another area used to hide illegal money. Ordinary people are subjected to laws that aim to prevent illegal money transactions, so why aren't larger enterprises watched as closely?

Some of the most well known banks in the world are also the biggest money launderers. The recent Troika Laundromat affair added another $8 billion to the trillions financial institutions wash every year. Over $2 trillion is laundered annually by criminals who utilize various ways to hide money in banks, which are often

"How the World's Leading Banks Help Launder $2 Trillion a Year," by Jamie Redman, Saint Bitts LLC, March 11, 2019, https://news.bitcoin.com/how-the-worlds-leading-banks-help-launder-2-trillion-a-year/. Reprinted by permission.

complicit or at least willing to turn a blind eye. The following is a look at money laundering schemes used by criminal enterprises that use the world's so-called "regulated" banks as their main laundromat system.

The World's "Regulated" Banks Wash More than $2 Trillion Every Year

Financial incumbents and politicians love to invade normal people's everyday activities and they'd love to know how our funds are being spent right down to the last penny. At the same time, the banking system that they regulate is used to wash trillions each and every year using schemes like shell companies, bogus supply chain invoices, smurfing, and "mirror" trades to hide funds that stem from illegal acts. In the last decade, few notable bankers or financiers have been jailed for financial crimes and money laundering save for Bernie Madoff. Many believe Madoff was only incarcerated because he stole from the banking cartel and shed light on their shady activities.

Washing Money Using Banks

Since the last financial crisis, dozens of the world's financial institutions have been caught laundering money and slapped with petty fines. Just recently the Troika Laundromat scandal revealed that banks like Citigroup, Deutsche Bank, and Raiffeisen helped criminals wash $8.8 billion in a seven-year period. Illicit funds are moved and obfuscated from the public eye using the traditional banking system in a variety of ingenious ways.

Mirror Trading

Mirror trading is a financial strategy that is legal in certain jurisdictions. The mirroring method allows two identical trades to be executed, but the selected strategy of the two combined trades cancels each other out. However, funds are still moved from one location to the next using the scheme. As one Quora commenter explains:

A client opens up a trading account with Deutsche Bank in Moscow. The client deposits let's say the equivalent of $10,000 in rubles in his account and asks the bank to buy that amount of blue chip shares on the Moscow stock exchange. The client has previously instructed the bank that the same shares are sold on the London stock exchange for GBP; both trades are executed within fractions of a second of each other. Voila. Clean as a whistle.

Back in 2017, Deutsche Bank paid more than $670 million in penalties for participating in mirror trades that stemmed from illegal activities in Russia. Money laundering scandals have proliferated at Deutsche Bank and the institution has paid more than $9 billion in fines since 2008. Many other well-known financial institutions have been caught assisting mirror trading offenses like Bank of America, J.P. Morgan, and Danske Bank Estonia.

Smurfing

Another popular move by banks is a method of laundering money known as "structuring" or "smurfing." This involves conducting a large number of small transactions through a regulated bank, usually in a specific pattern to avoid triggering anti-money laundering alarms. Lots of banks located around the world have been caught smurfing or allowing customers to smurf. For instance, in 2017 the Commonwealth Bank Australia was accused of 53,700 structuring related instances by Australia's financial watchdogs. In 2015 the Supreme Court in Vancouver charged the Canadian Imperial Bank of Commerce for assisting such transactions and there are countless other financial institutions that are simply dubbed "smurf banks."

Shell Companies

When people want to move shady money, lots of times they set up a fake business in order to hide the illegal proceeds. On some occasions, there are businesses that actually have operations like selling goods and services to obfuscate the illicit funds. But often, individuals set up "shell" companies, which are basically incorporated or limited liability firms only on paper with no real operation inside them.

According to the group of journalists who unveiled the Troika Laundromat scandal, roughly 75 shell firms were created to help facilitate the process. In the spring of 2017, it was also revealed that about 21 shell companies were involved in a money-laundering scheme that took place between 2010 and 2014 that involved washing $21 billion in illicit funds. That particular escapade involved the use of the world's top 50 banks including Credit Suisse, Deutsche Bank, Citibank, HSBC, Bank of China, and Royal Bank of Scotland.

Legitimate and Illegal Business Mixing

Just like the shell company example above, many banks have assisted people in mixing "dirty money" with legitimate business practices. There are all types of sanctioned businesses people use to mix illegal funds with an authorized entity and one of the biggest schemes uses real estate. Many well-known financial incumbents have been caught red-handed assisting with the mixing of real estate sales and illegal proceeds.

Selling properties and the real estate market, in general, is less scrutinized and in 2018 Denmark's largest bank was accused of mixing clean and dirty money through the sale of properties. Another way criminals and politicians use banks to launder money is through the use of casinos and legal gambling. Back in 2014, the Department of Justice's (DoJ) "Operation Choke Point" subpoenaed 50 banks in a casino money laundering ring in Las Vegas. The DoJ explained that banks like Wells Fargo, J.P. Morgan Chase & Co, and Bank of America were among the financial institutions involved.

While the Banks Wash Trillions and Get Slapped With Paltry Fines, Law Enforcement Focus on Petty Cash and Bitcoin Sales

Financial regulators and law enforcement agencies around the world seem obsessed with busting normal people for moving small amounts of funds. Police and three-letter agencies dedicate a lot of energy toward ordinary citizens who move bitcoin or petty cash, but allow bankers to wash trillions without jail. Last year Rustem Kazazi, a US citizen, had his life savings stolen ($58,100) from law enforcement and the TSA and Border Patrol at Cleveland Hopkins International Airport never charged him with a crime. In May 2017, entrepreneur Sal Mansy of Detroit, Michigan was charged by the DoJ and the District of Maine for selling bitcoins in an unlicensed manner. In fact, many Localbitcoins sellers have been prosecuted in the US for being an illegal money transmitter and hit with money laundering charges.

Unfortunately, the world's bureaucracy continues to focus on banning cash and claiming cryptocurrency's main form of use is money laundering. In reality, the central banks' fiat money with currencies like the US dollar and Japanese yen are the main vehicles for hiding shady funds. The status quo's banking institutions are the main facilitators of these crimes and the magnitude of money they hide eclipses the entire cryptocurrency market cap by a long shot.

8

Drug Trafficking and Money Laundering

Bruce Zagaris and Scott Ehlers

Bruce Zagaris is the editor and founder of International Enforcement Law Reporter *and a partner at the law firm of Berliner, Corcoran & Rowe. Scott Ehlers directs research at the Campaign for New Drug Policies.*

A staggering amount of money is being illegally exchanged in the drug trade, and drug traffickers need to find a way to transfer this money into legal form. Money laundering schemes fill this criminal need. Many laws have been enacted to expose this illegal activity and various US agencies are tasked with enforcing these laws. However, even with the best intentions problems plague the attempts of governments to prevent money laundering, some of which are engrained in the US Constitution and legal system. Problems with these attempts—as well as potential solutions—are explored in this viewpoint. Though the viewpoint was originally published in 1998 and various changes have been made in domestic and foreign policy since then, the essential nature of the problem of drug trafficking and money laundering remains much the same.

The trade in illicit drugs is estimated to be worth $400 billion a year, and it accounts for 8% of all international trade, according to the United Nations.

"Drug Trafficking & Money Laundering," by Bruce Zagaris and Scott Ehlers, Institute for Policy Studies, January 6, 1998. https://fpif.org/drug_trafficking_and_money_laundering/. Licensed under CC BY 3.0 US.

Key Points

- Drug traffickers seek to transform the monetary proceeds from their criminal activity into revenue with an apparently legal source. This is known as money laundering.
- Drug profits moving through the US financial system are estimated to be as high as $100 billion a year.
- Many countries have criminalized money laundering and instituted banking regulations to deter money laundering and make it easier to detect and seize the assets of criminal activity.

The trade in illicit drugs is estimated to be worth $400 billion a year, and it accounts for 8% of all international trade, according to the United Nations. In order to invest the profits of their illicit activities and avoid having their assets seized by the government, drug traffickers must transform the monetary proceeds from their criminal activity into revenue from apparently legal sources. This is known as money laundering.

In a May 1998 speech, President Clinton declared, "Up to $500 billion in criminal proceeds every single year—more than the GNP of most nations—is laundered, disguised as legitimate revenue, and much of it moves across our borders." As much as $100 billion a year in drug trafficking cash moves through the US financial system, according to the Financial Crimes Enforcement Network (FinCEN).

Though there are many ways to launder drug money, the process generally involves three basic stages. The first stage, "placement," entails disposal of the drug proceeds into domestic banks and foreign financial institutions. The second stage, "layering," moves funds between multiple financial institutions to hide their source and ownership and to disguise the audit trail. This can involve wire transfers or shell companies in offshore havens. In the third stage, "integration," a legitimate explanation for the funds is created. This can be done, for instance, via front companies, false invoicing, purchase of financial instruments (stocks, bonds, and certificates of deposit), or investment in real estate, tourism, and other legitimate businesses.

Innumerable schemes have been devised to hide the large sums of currency that are generated by illicit drug sales. One method, "structuring," involves breaking up large amounts of cash into transactions that amount to less than $10,000 to avoid currency-reporting requirements.

At present, the Colombian Black Market Peso Exchange method "is the single most efficient and extensive money laundering 'system' in the Western Hemisphere," according to FinCEN. The system involves Colombian traffickers who sell their dollar profits at a discount to agents in the US who work for peso brokers in Colombia. Once the dollars are delivered to the US-based agent, the Colombian broker deposits the agreed-upon funds in pesos in the traffickers' account. The broker assumes the risk of introducing the laundered funds into the US banking system and later sells the inventory of dollars to Colombian importers who bring in various legal goods, such as cigarettes or computers.

Other laundering schemes involve casinos, gems and precious metals, wire transfer companies, and smuggling currency out of the United States. Money launderers also use various offshore banking havens such as Panama, the Cayman Islands, the Bahamas, Aruba, Liechtenstein, and the Isle of Man.

Between 1970 and 1995, a series of US laws, regulations, and directives have sought to scrutinize movements of large cash transactions and suspicious financial activities. The Bank Secrecy Act (1970) obligates financial institutions to report cash transactions in excess of $10,000 using the Currency Transaction Report (CTR) and requires individuals to report the transportation of currency in excess of $5,000 (now $10,000) into or out of the United States.

The 1986 Money Laundering Control Act declared money laundering to be a crime in its own right and made "structuring"— transactions to avoid filing a CTR—a criminal offense. In 1995, Clinton signed Presidential Decision Directive 42, which freezes

US assets of Colombian drug trafficking organizations and bars US companies from doing business with the traffickers' front companies.

Various agencies (including the FBI, Customs, Drug Enforcement Administration, Internal Revenue Service, Federal Reserve Board, and Treasury) are responsible for enforcing money-laundering laws. FinCEN, a US Treasury division, uses artificial intelligence technology to analyze all CTRs and Suspicious Activity Reports filed by banks, thrifts, credit unions, and commercial and law enforcement databases.

Financial Intelligence Units (FIUs), similar to FinCEN, have been formed in many countries to obtain and process financial disclosure information and support anti-money-laundering efforts. Internationally, various national, regional, and global agreements and institutions (such as the Inter-American Drug Abuse Control Council of the Organization of American States) seek to combat money laundering. The 1988 UN Drug Convention also contains significant anti-money-laundering and asset-forfeiture provisions.

Problems with Current US Policy

Key Problems

- A wide variety of social factors ensure that drug trafficking and money laundering will continue to thrive for the foreseeable future.
- Money laundering is difficult to detect because of the high volume of banking transactions and because laundered transactions largely resemble legitimate commerce.
- The US Constitution, domestic privacy laws, and similar legal restraints in foreign countries impede the detection of money laundering.

In May 1998, President Clinton announced "a comprehensive international crime control strategy for America" in which he pledged to "seek new authority to fight money laundering and freeze the US assets of people arrested abroad."

Despite numerous laws, treaties, multilateral agreements, and public pronouncements, large-scale trafficking and money laundering continues because the demand is high, profits are enormous, and detection is difficult. Cocaine is produced for export at $950 to $1,235 a kilogram and sold at the wholesale level in the United States for $10,500 to $36,000 a kilogram. A kilogram of heroin costs about $3,000 to produce, but it sells wholesale in the US for $95,000 to $210,000. The average Colombian trafficking organization earns approximately $300 million annually, according to a 1994 State Department report.

Most illicit drugs are grown and processed in poor countries where economic opportunities are scarce, law enforcement is weak, and officials can be bribed or eliminated. Increasingly, as well, money laundering is also taking place in developing countries. "Measures in major financial markets to detect and prosecute laundering are driving it toward less developed markets linked to the global financial system," writes World Bank financial analyst David Scott.

The globalization of trade, finance, and communications has made it easier to transport illicit drugs and launder the proceeds. The sheer volume of financial transactions, many via wire transfers or electronic messages between banks, is staggering. Within the US, more than 465,000 wire transfers—valued at more than $2 trillion—are handled daily. Another 220,000 transfer messages are carried in and out of the United States by an international messaging system known as SWIFT (Society for Worldwide Interbank Financial Telecommunication).

In 1995, the Office of Technology Assessment (OTA) estimated that within the US approximately 0.05% of transfers (or roughly 250 transactions a day) involve money laundering.

Although a wire transfer initially contains information about the sender or "originator" of the transfer, as the transfer passes through several banks before reaching the beneficiary's account, the identification of the originator is often dropped. Under regulations instituted in 1996, US banks are required to identify the originator and the beneficiary of wire transfers, and such information must travel with the message throughout the transfer. But foreign banks are not required to supply this information.

Several services offered by international banks have been used by launderers. "Private banking," a little known and largely unregulated service, has been offered by Citicorp, Chase, and other US financial institutions. It provides what Congresswoman Maxine Waters (D-CA) describes as a "'don't ask, don't tell' policy toward their wealthiest, and sometimes dirtiest, clients."

This service can involve offshore accounts, moving large sums of money from one country to another, devising intricate networks of accounts, and helping to purchase homes, businesses, and investments with laundered funds. The service can also include setting up "concentration accounts," where funds from various individuals are commingled and their origins not identified. Citibank's private banking service, for instance, laundered tens of millions of dollars in drug money for Raul Salinas, the jailed brother of former Mexican President Carlos Salinas.

Although the US is one of the world's leading money laundering centers, very few money laundering cases are actually filed—an indication that this crime is difficult to detect and/or that inadequate resources are being devoted to enforcement. In 1995, only 62 criminal money-laundering cases were filed with US attorneys, of the 138 defendants, 52 were convicted.

In May 1998, however, the Justice and Treasury departments announced the successful culmination of "Operation Casablanca," hailed as "the largest, most comprehensive drug money laundering case in the history of US law enforcement." The three-year sting operation (involving some 200 undercover agents) led to the arrest of 26 Mexican bank officials, the seizure of an estimated $150 million, and the freezing of over 100 bank accounts in the United States and Europe.

The US accused three of Mexico's largest banks and the Colombia branch of Price Waterhouse, a major international auditing firm headquartered in New York, of knowingly aiding

Juárez (Mexico) and Cali (Colombia) drug cartels in laundering hundreds of millions of dollars of their US drug sales. Mexican officials said they were jointly (with the US) investigating another 260 cases of alleged money laundering.

But the detection of money laundering is impeded by various national laws that protect financial, communication, and data privacy. In the United States, the Right to Financial Privacy Act of 1978 provides many of the procedural protections for financial records guaranteed more broadly by the Fourth Amendment. The Electronic Communications Privacy Act of 1986 essentially prohibits the monitoring of wire transfers while in transit or in storage without a court order, warrant, or administrative subpoena.

In a significant number of countries, bank secrecy laws hinder obtaining comprehensive information about financial transactions by prohibiting banking officials from releasing customer information to persons outside the financial institution, or simply by prohibiting access by foreign law enforcement agencies on the grounds of national sovereignty. Additionally, under data protection laws such as the European Union's Data Protection Directive, information may be prohibited from leaving a signatory country if it is being sent to a country with less stringent data protection laws.

Toward a New Foreign Policy

Key Recommendations

- Strengthen domestic and international anti-money-laundering cooperation and regulations.
- Increase funding for treatment, prevention, and economic development programs in both the US and source countries to reduce drug production, sales, consumption, and trafficking.
- Revise the UN Conventions on Illicit Drugs to permit governments to experiment in the regulated distribution of currently illicit drugs.

Although various international standards have been written to guide governments in adopting anti-money-laundering policies, not all jurisdictions have implemented regulations. Those countries that have not implemented these standards should be encouraged to do so to reduce money laundering activity.

In the US, regulations and procedures for banks and other financial institutions need to be tightened and controlled. There also needs to be more vigorous prosecution of banks and banking officials who knowingly assist in and profit from money-laundering operations. Objecting to the mammoth financial merger of Citibank/Citicorp and Travelers Group, Rep. Maxine Waters, introduced amendments to the 1998 Financial Services Act that would:

- Require the Federal Reserve Board (when reviewing bank merger applications) to evaluate a company's anti-money-laundering efforts and refuse to allow a merger if one of the companies is under investigation, is being prosecuted, or has been found civilly or criminally liable for a money laundering offense;
- Require any bank engaging in private banking activities to file yearly reports describing the procedures used in these operations and how the bank was complying with federal anti-money-laundering laws; and,
- Prohibit concentration accounts, which have been known to be utilized by money launderers.

The laundering of drug proceeds can be reduced through the implementation and strengthening of anti-money-laundering standards, but these regulations can only have a limited effect on curtailing money laundering. In 1995, the Office of Technology Assessment analyzed the feasibility of implementing a massive data surveillance system that could serve as an "automated informant" for suspicious activity. The OTA found the system would not work because the number of money laundering transactions is believed to be relatively small, limited information is contained in wire transfers, and it is difficult to characterize a "typical" money laundering transaction, rendering identification and profiling very problematic. Such a system would also pose a serious threat to privacy and constitutional protections.

Rather than simply focusing on implementing more laws to fight money laundering and drug trafficking, greater emphasis should be placed on addressing the fundamental causes of the problem—namely, the demand for drugs and a lack of economic opportunities in both developing countries and US urban centers. In the US, more emphasis should be placed on treatment, prevention, and urban development in an effort to reduce drug demand and sales. This would, in effect, reduce the proceeds to drug traffickers.

Although drug trafficking and money laundering will be reduced if demand for illicit drugs is reduced in consumer countries and if alternative forms of development are implemented in source and transit countries, drug consumption will continue to exist. The artificially high profits of supplying drug consumers serve to impede alternative forms of development.

The illicit drug trade funds powerful criminal organizations, resulting in widespread corruption, violence, and an undermining of the rule of law. This, in turn, impedes the prosecution of these organizations, weakens the judicial system, and prevents the effective implementation of anti-money-laundering controls in the banking system. Weak legal structures and social instability also thwart legal commercial development.

Ultimately, the UN Conventions on Illicit Drugs (1961, 1971, 1988) must be revised to allow for signatory parties to experiment in regulating the distribution and sale of certain illicit drugs if the problems created by prohibition are to be addressed. Unfortunately, recent actions by the UN make it clear that such experiments will not be considered. A new UN counter-drug plan proposed to the 1998 General Assembly Special Session on Illicit Drugs is useful in promoting crop substitution programs, but it sets the wholly unrealistic goal of eradicating the world's entire production of heroin, cocaine, and marijuana by the year 2008.

There are a variety of regulation schemes that could be implemented to control access to drugs while removing the profits from criminal enterprises. Ideally, the aim should be to minimize the harm that drugs cause to users and society at large, to shrink the size of the black market, and to obviate the need to launder illicit funds.

9

Money Laundering in Online Gambling

David Sheldon

David Sheldon is the Editor-in-Chief at Casino.org.

As the online gaming industry continues to grow, so too does the amount of money that is laundered through it. Money launderers have always made use of casinos and gambling in their schemes, but the ease and relative anonymity of online gambling make it an even more attractive option. In 2018 the UK Gambling Commission reprimanded five online casinos for not doing enough to prevent money laundering—a sign that more must be done to prevent crime on these websites. The viewpoint also examines the role of cryptocurrencies and micro-laundering in multi-player online role-playing games and how they fit into money laundering schemes.

G ambling has always been a magnet to people intent on processing the proceeds of crime—in short, money laundering.

This is an industry characterized by huge sums of money moving from place to place at dazzling speed.

The potential for it to be used as a vehicle for transforming filthy lucre into untraceable, clean cash will always be there.

However, law enforcement agencies are more determined than ever to tackle crime by cracking down on money laundering. And many have their sights firmly trained on betting operators.

"How Money Laundering Works in Online Gambling," by David Sheldon, Editor-in-Chief at Casino.org. Reprinted by permission.

The UK Gambling Commission warned five online casinos in 2018 they could lose their licenses. They were not doing enough, the commission said, to stop criminals using their websites to launder money.

But whatever measures the authorities and betting operators impose, the online gaming market is now worth $170billion a year.

That makes the challenge to eradicate money laundering a huge one—and means the temptation for criminals to use it for that purpose remains equally large.

So, How Does Money Laundering Work?

Money laundering is a process by which criminals transform the proceeds of their activity into legitimate cash.

Once money has been laundered, it is hard for law enforcement bodies to trace it as having been obtained through criminal activity.

There are three stages in a typical money laundering process:

1. **Placement:** The act of depositing money (such as the cash proceeds of a drug deal) into the financial system.
2. **Layering:** The source of the proceeds is disguised by creating complex layers of financial transactions to obscure any audit trail.
3. **Integration:** The laundered money is integrated into the legitimate financial system.

How Does Money Laundering Take Place Through Online Gambling?

The online market now comprises more than one-third of the UK gambling industry. The amounts of cash flowing through digital sportsbooks' and online casinos' coffers are astronomical.

One strategy favored by money launderers is to deposit a large amount of money in a betting account. They then place a few small bets for appearances' sake, before emptying the whole account.

This process is even harder to detect if the criminals are patient enough to break their loot down into small amounts.

They can then set up dozens of betting accounts, with deposits well below a benchmark likely to attract attention. After a short while, they withdraw their money.

In these instances, any paper trail will look innocent and legitimate.

The FBI has admitted that even licensed sites offer an opportunity to transfer high volumes of money in and out of different accounts.

And this is an industry in which dozens of unlicensed sites are launched every day—some of them in jurisdictions with weak or non-existent supervisory regimes.

How Is It Different from Standard Money Laundering?

The International Monetary Fund has estimated that a staggering $1.5trillion is laundered every year—that's 5% of the world's GDP.

Even if only a small fraction of this amount is laundered through online gambling, it means tens of millions of dollars change hands illegally each year.

Money laundering through online gambling is extremely similar to the standard process.

If anything, it is harder to detect because using the money to have a few bets gives a convincing veneer of legitimacy.

In the hands of a shrewd gambler whose losses to a sportsbook or online casino are small, a criminal could even launder their entire stash. They would lose only a few percentage points – a better rate than they'd have to pay to an old-fashioned back-street money launderer.

How the Gambling Industry Has Responded So Far

The Gambling Commission revealed in a 2018 report that it had found money laundering reporting officers who couldn't explain what constitutes money laundering.

This was in the same year as the Commission warned five casinos they could lose their license (see above).

It was also in 2018 that William Hill, one of the biggest names in UK bookmaking, was fined £6.2million for what the Commission called "systemic failures" regarding money laundering.

Lack of proper checks meant 10 customers could deposit large sums that were the result of crime.

The Commission's advice includes the development of systems and controls to reduce the risk posed by money laundering.

But organizations have to do more than that.

They have to be committed to them, assess them regularly and train employees to check customers and know what constitutes suspicious activity.

In response, the gambling industry has been tightening up its act. Online casinos, for instance, are now obliged to verify the identity of players and to maintain an audit trail that tracks the source of money placed in bets.

How Big a Risk Is Cryptocurrency?

Everybody thinks they know two things about cryptocurrency. It's anonymous, and transactions are smooth between accounts and across national borders.

On the face of it, with more and more online casinos accepting Bitcoin and other cryptocurrencies, that should make it a haven for money launderers.

However, cryptocurrencies are no longer as anonymous as they used to be. And one significant deterrent to people looking to invest ill-gotten gains is that it's not always easy to liquidate your crypto-assets.

What Is Micro-laundering?

Micro-laundering operates in the same way as money laundering. The three main steps of placement, layering and integration are identical.

But Jean-Loup Richet, a cyber-crime researcher at Harvard University, conducted an in-depth study into micro-laundering through games.

He found criminals leaned towards using multi-player online role-playing games such as Second Life and World of Warcraft. He called them "an easy way for criminals to launder money."

Micro-laundering follows a three-step process:

1. Purchase credits (or gold, as gamers call them) using pre-paid or stolen cards.
2. Set up a shop on a gold-selling site. These are popular with large numbers of gamers.
3. A buyer purchases gold and the launderer cleans his illegal money. Neither the buyer or seller is aware of each other's identity.

The sheer volume of high-speed transactions makes it extremely difficult to spot micro-laundering.

What's Next for the Online Gambling Industry?

Sarah Harrison, CEO of the Gambling Commission, has warned its members: "It is vital that the gambling industry takes its duty to protect customers and keep crime out of gambling seriously."

All members of the commission have responsibilities under the Proceeds of Crime Act 2002. They must report any knowledge, or even suspicion, that a customer is using the proceeds of crime to gamble.

As well as warning five casinos they could lose their licenses, the commission spoke of the "serious nature" of its findings on a host of other operators' controls against money laundering.

Quite simply, anyone who sets themselves up in business as a legitimate gambling operation has both a legal and a moral responsibility to do everything to reassure its customers and the regulators.

Like many industries, the issue of credibility is central to the success of online gambling operations.

If customers fear they are betting alongside people using the industry to launder the proceeds of criminal activities, they will go elsewhere.

What should really sharpen the focus of online operators is the fact that their responsibilities are not only legal and moral, but commercial too.

10

Cryptocurrency Scams Pass as Legitimate Businesses

Nir Kshetri

Nir Kshetri is a professor at the University of North Carolina at Greensboro. His writing has appeared in Scientific American, *the* Wall Street Journal, *and* Christian Science Monitor, *among others.*

The cryptocurrency market is rife with schemers and scammers just waiting to cash in on unsuspecting people who want to make money through investing in cryptocurrencies and believe they are investing in legitimate businesses. Using social media and digital platforms, cryptocurrency fraudsters are cashing in. People are being tricked into thinking their money will offer better returns if they buy into cryptocurrencies, and some schemes make it difficult to tell whether investors are actually getting good returns on their investments. But ultimately, fraudsters are getting rich while innocent people are losing big sums of money.

Millions of cryptocurrency investors have been scammed out of massive sums of real money. In 2018, losses from cryptocurrency-related crimes amounted to US$1.7 billion. The criminals use both old-fashioned and new-technology tactics to swindle their marks in schemes based on digital currencies exchanged through online databases called blockchains.

From researching blockchain, cryptocurrency and cybercrime, I can see that some cryptocurrency fraudsters rely on tried-and-true Ponzi schemes that use income from new participants to pay out returns to earlier investors.

Others use highly automatized and sophisticated processes, including automated software that interacts with Telegram, an internet-based instant-messaging system popular among people interested in cryptocurrencies. Even when a cryptocurrency plan is legitimate, fraudsters can still manipulate its price in the marketplace.

An even more basic question arises, though: How are unsuspecting investors attracted to cryptocurrency frauds in the first place?

Fast-Talking Swindlers

Some cryptocurrency fraudsters appeal to people's greed, promising big returns. For example, an unknown group of entrepreneurs runs the scam bot iCenter, which is a Ponzi scheme for Bitcoin and Litecoin. It doesn't provide information on investment strategies, but somehow promises investors 1.2% daily returns.

The iCenter scheme operates through a group chat on Telegram. It starts with a small group of scammers who are in on the racket. They get a referral code that they share with others, in blogs and on social media, hoping to get them to join the chat. Once there, the newcomers see encouraging and exciting messages from the original scammers. Some newcomers decide to invest, at which point they are assigned an individual bitcoin wallet, into which they can deposit bitcoins. They agree to wait some period of time—99 or 120 days—to receive a significant return.

During that time, the newcomers often use social media to share their own referral codes with friends and contacts, bringing more people into the group chat and into the investment scheme. There's no actual investment of the funds in any legitimate business. Instead, when new people join, the person who recruited them gets a percentage of the new funds, and the cycle continues, paying out to earlier participants from each round of newer investors.

Some members work especially hard to bring in new funds, posting tutorial videos and pictures of themselves holding large amounts of money as enticements to join the scam.

Lies and More Lies

Some scammers go for straight-up deception. The founders of scam cryptocurrency OneCoin defrauded investors of $3.8 billion by convincing people their nonexistent cryptocurrency was real.

Other scams are based on impressing potential victims with jargon or claims of specialized knowledge. The Global Trading scammers claimed they took advantage of price differences on various cryptocurrency exchanges to profit from what is called arbitrage—simply buying cheaply and selling at higher prices. Really they just took investors' money.

Global Trading used a bot on Telegram, too—investors could send a balance inquiry message and get a response with false information about how much was in their account, sometimes even seeing balances climb by 1% in an hour. With returns looking like that, who could blame people for sharing the scheme with their friends and family on social media?

Exploiting Friends and Family

Once a scheme has started, it stays alive—at least for a while— through social media. One person gets taken in by the promise of big returns on cryptocurrency investments and spreads the word to friends and family members.

Sometimes big names get involved. For instance, the kingpin behind GainBitcoin and other alleged scams in India convinced a number of Bollywood celebrities to promote his book, "Cryptocurrency for Beginners." He even tried to make himself a bit of a celebrity, proclaiming himself a "cryptocurrency guru," as he led efforts that cost investors between $769 million and $2 billion.

Not all the celebrities know they're involved. In one blog post, iCenter featured a video that purported to be an endorsement by Dwayne "The Rock" Johnson, holding a sign featuring iCenter's logo. Videos of Justin Timberlake and Christopher Walken were deceptively edited so they appeared to praise iCenter, too.

Fraudulent Initial Coin Offerings

Another popular scam technique is called an "initial coin offering." A potentially legitimate investment opportunity, an initial coin offering essentially is a way for a startup cryptocurrency company to raise money from its future users: In exchange for sending active cryptocurrencies like bitcoin and ethereum, customers are promised a discount on the new cryptocoins.

Many initial coin offerings have turned out to be scams, with organizers engaging in cunning plots, even renting fake offices and creating fancy-looking marketing materials. In 2017, a lot of hype and media coverage about cryptocurrencies fed a huge wave of initial coin offering fraud. In 2018, about 1,000 initial coin offering efforts collapsed, costing backers at least $100 million. Many of these projects had no original ideas—more than 15% of them had copied ideas from other cryptocurrency efforts, or even plagiarized supporting documentation.

Investors looking for returns in a new technology sector are still interested in blockchains and cryptocurrencies—but should beware that they are complex systems that are new even to those who are selling them. Newcomers and relative experts alike have fallen prey to scams.

In an environment like the current cryptocurrency market, potential investors should be very careful to research what they're putting their money into and be sure to find out who is involved as well as what the actual plan is for making real mone —without defrauding others.

11

Money Laundering May Be Easier in the Digital World

Alexon Bell

Alexon Bell has worked as an expert monitoring financial crimes and anti-money laundering systems. He is cofounder and head of Quantexa, which provides clients with comprehensive anti-money laundering systems.

The rise of the digital world has its advantages and has made life better in many respects, but in one area it has failed miserably. Digital convenience through social media, online shopping and banking, and even online services such as Airbnb and Uber have made it possible for criminals to fleece the public. In some instances, unknowing individuals have become involved in money laundering schemes without their consent—people lured by cash and luxury items posted on social media have let criminals use their bank accounts in the hopes of big money payoffs or the promise of receiving high-price luxury goods.

The rise of social media, peer-to-peer platforms and online banks has had a huge impact on the convenience and ease of transactions between individuals. But these platforms have simultaneously opened new doors for fraudsters to trick people out of their money and particularly criminals looking for ever more innovative ways of laundering the proceeds of their crimes.

"Is money laundering easier in a digital world?" by Alexon Bell, Future Publishing Limited, May 10, 2018. Reprinted by permission.

In an increasingly digital world, is money laundering becoming easier to pull off?

New Forms of Money Laundering

With ecommerce so commonplace and only on the rise, legitimate websites are being used as payment processors in order to launder vast amounts of money. Drugs can be ordered online and the transaction will appear as something innocuous on your statement, such as a floristry purchase. From the bank's side, their customer appears to be an online florist, helping mask funds as cash is not used. Transactions are funnelled through other legitimate payment ecosystems for illegitimate purposes, including the financing of terror through criminal enterprises. Last year it was alleged that an ISIS operative in the US had used eBay to "sell" computer printers and received payments for these transactions from overseas via PayPal.

Peer-to-Peer Marketplaces

The sharing economy is on the rise and some of the most recognisable peer-to-peer brands are being exploited through their online payment systems. The nature of a peer-to-peer marketplace enables direct transactions from criminals on one side and complicit players on the other side, thus laundering money through a legitimate platform. The ease of use of these apps and websites is fuelling such activity, and their popularity and global adoption allows criminals to hide amongst huge volumes of transactions between lay people.

Last year, it was discovered that Airbnb had been exploited by money launderers, with criminals booking fake stays in rooms with complicit Airbnb hosts. Such a scheme works by criminals using stolen credit cards to book rooms through the peer-to-peer marketplace and paying for their fake stay online —with complicit hosts closing the loop. The transaction turns criminal proceeds into ostensibly legitimate earnings. News sources claimed that online Russian forums were being used to connect criminals to complicit hosts. In many instances these funds were laundered across borders, allowing the money to be hidden even more effectively.

A similar scheme was recently reported in which Uber was being used to launder criminal proceeds through fake transactions. In this system, middle men use stolen credit cards to book fake rides which never actually happen, with complicit drivers. A cut is taken by the drivers and the middle men, leaving the rest of the now seemingly legitimate funds to the client.

Both these recent examples show the ease with which sharing economy marketplaces can be exploited. The current systems to police thousands of peer-to-peer transactions across the globe, monitoring transactions and flagging any suspicious activity, simply aren't strong enough to spot scams that look very similar to the sea of legitimate interactions.

Social Media

Social media has an increasingly dominant role to play in recruiting people to facilitate money laundering—whether they do so knowingly or unknowingly. Several recent reports have highlighted young people being recruited as money mules though social media. Last week, fraud prevention body, Cifas published their annual report, revealing that in 2017 there were 32,000 cases of 14 to 24 year olds allowing their bank accounts to be used to move the proceeds of crime—an increase of 27 per cent. Social media is fuelling the spread of images of young people with cash and luxury items, luring young people into schemes which promise to get them rich quick. Unwitting mules are also being recruited through social media offers of fake jobs or initiatives to make extra money. Messaging app WhatsApp is being used as a communication method with these young mules or victims.

Scale of the Issue

Online platforms are an attractive option for money launderers due to their global reach, speed, low cost and simplicity. There is no need to create a fake "shop front" or false identities and no goods need to be moved.

Online money laundering is only set to grow. Global retail e-commerce sales are estimated to top $2.2 trillion annually, providing greater opportunities for criminals to hide their laundering activities among high volumes of legitimate transactions. Likewise, the popularity of cryptocurrencies and alternative payment platforms are garnering growing criticism and concerns over the transparency of transactions and the potential for easier than ever money laundering.

A Digital Solution

The digital world we live in is opening new doors for criminals to launder their money in different and creative ways. Only a digital-first approach will help tackle the issue.

New and ground-breaking innovations in technology that monitor transactions are helping to identify suspicious behaviour and patterns amongst huge numbers of legitimate payments and interactions. In particular, monitoring software is being used to put transactions in their proper context: making links and connections between parties and their transactions, using internal as well as external data sources. This contextual monitoring approach helps companies to see a 360° view of their customers—making it easier to identify unusual and illegitimate transactions consistently and accurately amongst thousands of genuine interactions. Using a combination of this digitally compiled insight and human intelligence will challenge online money laundering with a digital-first approach.

Peer-to-peer platforms, online payments and banking, and social media have been adopted across the globe thanks to their convenience, speed and ease of use. However, it is exactly these qualities that criminals are increasingly exploiting to support illegitimate activity.

While technology is fuelling this new approach to money laundering, technology is also the solution. Just as the criminal spheres of fraud and money laundering are converging, many organisations see the solution as a fusion of human intelligence with Artificial Intelligence. The key is cutting through the noise.

12

The European Union Backs Stronger Anti–Money Laundering Laws

European Commission

The European Commission (EC) is the executive body of the European Union. The EC is comprised of various commissioners, one per member state. It oversees laws and treaties proposed and implemented by the European Union.

The European Commission has adopted a stance that supports continued efforts to crack down on money laundering and the financing of terrorism through money laundering. Rules exist across the European Union to counter criminal activity. The Commission stresses that the laws that are already in place need to be enforced equally across all EU countries. The Commission further suggests ways to implement agreed-upon legislation and best practices to prevent money laundering and terrorist activities, and will continue to guide the European Union to achieve these goals.

The European Commission is today adopting a Communication and four reports that will support European and national authorities in better addressing money laundering and terrorist financing risks. The Juncker Commission put strong EU rules in place with the fourth and the fifth Anti-Money laundering directives and reinforced the supervisory role of the European

"Fight against money laundering and terrorist financing: Commission assesses risks and calls for better implementation of the rules," European Commission, July 24, 2019. Reprinted by permission.

Banking Authority. The reports stress the need for their full implementation while underlining that a number of structural shortcomings in the implementation of the Union's anti-money laundering and counter terrorist financing rules still need to be addressed. Today's package will serve as a basis for future policy choices on how to further strengthen the EU anti-money laundering framework.

Frans Timmermans, First Vice-President said:

We must close off all opportunities for criminals and terrorists to abuse our financial system and threaten the security of Europeans. There are some very concrete improvements which can be made quickly at operational level. The Commission will continue to support Member States in this, whilst also reflecting on how to address the remaining structural challenges.

Valdis Dombrovskis, Vice-President for the Euro and Social Dialogue, also in charge of Financial Stability, Financial Services and Capital Markets Union, said:

A credible framework for preventing and fighting money laundering and terrorist financing is essential to maintain the integrity of the European financial system and reduce risks to financial stability. Yet, today's analysis gives more proof that our strong AML rules have not been equally applied in all banks and all EU countries. So we have a structural problem in the Union's capacity to prevent that the financial system is used for illegitimate purposes. This problem has to be addressed and solved sooner rather than later.

Věra Jourová, Commissioner for Justice, Consumers and Gender Equality said:

We have stringent anti-money laundering rules at EU level, but we need all Member States to implement these rules on the ground. We don't want to see any weak link point in the EU that criminals could exploit. The recent scandals have shown that Member States should treat this as a matter of urgency.

The *Towards a better implementation of the EU's anti-money laundering and countering the financing of terrorism framework* Communication gives an overview of the four reports published today: the supranational risk assessment report provides an update of sectorial risks associated with money laundering and terrorist financing. The assessment of recent high-profile money laundering cases in the financial sector, the Financial Intelligence Units and the interconnection of central bank account registries' reports analyse the shortcomings in current anti-money laundering supervision and cooperation, and identifies ways to address them.

Assessment of Money Laundering Risks Across the Internal Market

The supranational risk assessment report is a tool to help Member States identify and address money laundering and terrorist financing risks. It is adopted every two years by the Commission since 2017.

The report shows that most recommendations of the first supranational risk assessment have been implemented by the various actors. However, some horizontal vulnerabilities remain, particularly with regard to anonymous products, the identification of beneficial owners and new unregulated products such as virtual assets. Some of these will be addressed by the upcoming transposition of the fifth Anti-Money Laundering Directive. The report also recalls that Member States still have to fully transpose the fourth Anti-money laundering directive. The Commission calls upon Member States to implement the directive fully and follow the recommendations of this report. This would improve cooperation between supervisors, raise awareness among obliged entities and provide further guidance on beneficial ownership identification.

Assessment and Lessons from Recent Money Laundering Cases

Following a number of exchanges with the European Parliament and a request from the Council in December 2018, the European Commission has analysed ten recent publicly known cases of money laundering in EU banks to provide an analysis of some of the current shortcomings and outline a possible way forward.

While not being exhaustive, the report shows that:

- Banks, in a number of the cases analysed, did not respect effectively or sometimes did not comply at all with anti-money laundering requirements. They lacked the right internal mechanisms to prevent money laundering and did not align their anti-money laundering/counter terrorism financing policies when they had risky business models. The findings also highlighted a lack of coordination between such policies, either at the level of individual entities or at group level.

- National authorities responded with significant differences in terms of the timeliness and effectiveness of their supervisory actions. There were major divergences in terms of prioritisation, resources, expertise and available tools. More particularly with respect to the supervision of a banking group, the supervisors had a tendency to rely excessively on the anti-money laundering framework of host Member States and this impinged on the effectiveness of supervisory actions in cross-border cases at EU level. In addition, the division of responsibilities led to ineffective cooperation between anti-money laundering authorities, prudential authorities, Financial Intelligence Units and law enforcement authorities.

These deficiencies point to outstanding structural issues in the implementation of EU rules, which have been addressed only in part. The regulatory and supervisory fragmentation, coupled with the diversity of tasks, powers and tools available to public authorities, create weaknesses in the implementation of EU rules. Shortcomings in anti-money laundering policies and supervision are more prominent in cross-border situations, both within the EU but also in relation to non-EU countries. While significant actions have been taken by banks and supervisors, more remains to be done. There is, for instance, a need for further harmonisation across Member States and strengthened supervision.

The Need for Cooperation Between Financial Intelligence Units (FIU)

Financial Intelligence Units play a key role in identifying money laundering risks in each country. The EU FIU's Platform, which is an expert group of the Commission, has greatly improved the cooperation over the last years, but the Commission has identified remaining issues:

- **Access by FIUs to information:** due to their different status, powers, and organisation, some FIUs are not able to access and share relevant information (financial, administrative and law enforcement).
- **Information sharing** between FIUs remains insufficient and is often too slow.
- **IT tools:** FIUs also sometimes lack the proper IT tools to efficiently import and export information to/from the FIU. net.
- **Limited scope of the EU FIUs' Platform**, which cannot produce legally-binding templates, guidelines and standards.

The report suggests some concrete changes, such as a new support mechanism, that would further improve the cooperation between Financial Intelligence Units (FIU) across the EU.

Interconnection of Central Bank Account Registries

The report on the interconnection of central bank account registries sets out a number of elements to be considered for a possible interconnection of bank account registries and data retrieval systems. The Commission suggests that such a system could possibly be a decentralised system with a common platform at EU level. To achieve the interconnection, legislative action would be required, following consultation with Member States' governments, Financial Intelligence Units, law enforcement authorities and Asset Recovery Offices.

Next Steps

Today's reports will inform the future debate on further action in this area, including with regard to the obligations of financial institutions and the powers and tools necessary for effective supervision. The current degree of integration of the banking market will also require further work on the cross-border aspects of the anti-money laundering/terrorist financing framework. The Commission will continue to monitor closely the implementation of EU anti-money laundering rules by the Member States.

Background

Under the Juncker Commission, the EU has strengthened the anti-money laundering/ counter terrorist financing framework by adopting the fourth Anti-Money Laundering Directive that had to be transposed by Member States by June 2017. The Commission is assessing the transposition of the fourth Anti-Money Laundering Directive, while also working to verify that the rules are correctly implemented by Member States. The Commission has launched infringement procedures against a majority of Member States as it assessed that the communications received from the Member States did not represent a complete transposition of this Directive.

The fifth Anti-Money Laundering Directive will improve the powers of Financial Intelligence Units, increase the transparency around beneficial ownership information, as well as regulate virtual currencies and pre-paid cards to better prevent terrorist financing. Member States are due to transpose the Directive into national law by January 2020.

Following the uncovering of several money laundering cases in 2018, the Commission set up in May 2018 a joint working group together with the European Supervisory Authorities and the European Central Bank. On the basis of the working group's recommendations, the Commission issued in September 2018 a Communication on strengthening the AML and prudential frameworks and new rules to strengthen the role of the European Banking Authority. This led to the reinforcement of the anti-money laundering and terrorist financing dimension in prudential banking legislation through the adoption of the fifth Capital Requirements Directive in December 2018.

13

Global Action Needed Against Money Laundering

Nigel Gould-Davies

Nigel Gould-Davies is an associate fellow in the Russian and Euroasian program at Chatham House. He teaches at Mahidol University in Thailand and previously worked for the British Foreign Office. He is an expert in Russia policy and international energy politics, particularly in Southeast Asia.

Money laundering is a global activity, so transnational cooperation is needed to stop it. Some countries around the world still make it easy for owners of illegally attained wealth to hide it and transform it into legal forms. Money laundering is unlike other high profile crimes that cause public outcry. It's not like child pornography, human trafficking, or terrorism, but it still poses a serious threat to countries and institutions. The United States and UK are target countries for moving illegal funds and, consequently, these countries should increase their anti-corruption standards when it comes to financial transactions from other countries.

As an inherently transnational activity, global money-laundering is perhaps the definitive problem in need of cross-border, rules-based cooperation. The G7 should lead the way.

Every year, owners of illicit wealth send huge sums of money from the countries where they made it to jurisdictions where they

"Drive Global Action on Money-Laundering," by Dr. Nigel Gould-Davies, Chatham House, June 12, 2019. Reprinted by permission.

can conceal its origins. They can do so because laws, practices and intermediaries in the receiving countries make money-laundering safe and easy. These arrangements abet criminality, corruption and insecurity on a global scale. There is a clear, compelling and urgent case for closing this major governance gap.

Transnational organized crime has long relied on the ability to launder its earnings. But the issue goes much wider. Those who enrich themselves through corrupt relationships and tax evasion routinely send the proceeds to safer jurisdictions.[1] The scale of these outflows dwarfs international aid budgets designed to support good governance. The provision by receiving states of what are, in effect, corruption-protection services thus entrenches misgovernance.

Corrupt financial inflows also present a serious security threat by eroding financial integrity and international reputation. But this security dimension has been growing even more severe. Much corrupt money flows from countries that seek to undermine Western interests and values.

The ability of elites in those countries to send assets to, and conceal them in, the West sometimes helps sustain authoritarian regimes. Some illegal financial inflows are used to interfere in election campaigns, co-opt local interests or take stakes in strategic companies. Money-laundering is also used to evade sanctions imposed to punish unacceptable behaviour.[2]

Three steps are needed to make progress against international money-laundering. First, a universal norm of transparency needs to be established in respect of the beneficial ownership of corporate vehicles. Public registries of beneficial owners, bolstered with reliable data, must ensure that such owners are declared as natural persons, not legal entities.[3] These registries should be standardized and interconnected to facilitate cooperation.

Second, intermediaries need to be regulated effectively. These are the individuals and companies (banks, and trust and company service providers, or "obliged entities" in EU terminology) that conduct the financial, legal, accountancy, property and other administrative operations which enable money to enter a country.

Their customer due diligence should include, in particular, establishing the identity of the beneficial owners of the entities that they service.

Regulatory authorities should incentivize intermediaries to internalize a culture of compliance. Too often, compliance is formulaic and "tick-boxy." Compare this with best practice in high-physical-risk industries, such as oil and gas. Here, the best companies drive continuous safety improvement in every aspect of their operations. This commitment is part of their corporate culture. Financial, property and legal service providers should adopt a similar mindset in their management of compliance risk.

Third, implementation needs to be properly resourced. Effective and consistent enforcement even of current laws and regulations will yield significant gains. This will require a step change in budgets, personnel and skills. Unlike other transnational crimes that it facilitates, such as terrorism or human trafficking, money-laundering is rarely an emotive issue for public opinion.

Political leaders should therefore provide the drive, direction and resources needed to prioritize enforcement. They should also adequately fund research that supports effective policy with rigorous, evidence based analysis of the scale of the threat, the forms it takes, and the ways it is evolving.

Over the past decade, a global consensus has emerged that money-laundering should be addressed more effectively. In 2012 the Financial Action Task Force (FATF), the leading international standards-setter in this area, agreed new recommendations endorsed by nearly every country in the world.

Following this example, in 2014 the G20 adopted "High Level Principles on Beneficial Ownership Transparency." In 2015 and 2018, the EU agreed its 4th and 5th Money Laundering Directives. The latter requires member states to establish public registries of beneficial ownership for corporate and other legal entities by January 2020.

But recent revelations, from leaks and whistle-blowers, have brought home the continued severity of the problem. The

2016 Panama Papers investigation revealed multi-billion-dollar fraud, tax evasion and sanctions evasion hidden through offshore companies. In 2018 Danske Bank, Denmark's largest bank, was found to have processed $230 billion in suspicious transactions.[4]

Revelations from scandals such as these are likely to continue to emerge. They demonstrate that the rules governing financial inflows, and the resources devoted to their enforcement, remain inadequate in relation to the scale of the challenge.

The priority now is to focus on better outcomes by strengthening global norms, bringing national practices into line with them and, above all, developing the capacity to implement them. While this is a global challenge, Western countries should take the lead. They, and the jurisdictions they control (like the UK Overseas Territories and Crown Dependencies), are the major service providers for illicit transnational financial flows.

They also face the biggest security threats from regimes that transfer assets overseas. And Western progress will have a wider demonstration effect by undercutting excuses made by others for resisting higher standards. Established best practice can also provide the basis for peer assistance and technical support to other states.

The most attractive destinations of all for illicit money are the US and the UK, with their highly developed financial and facilitation industries, traditions of light-touch regulation and strong rule of law. Their G7 presidencies in 2020 and 2021 respectively are a natural opportunity to demonstrate sustained global leadership in efforts to counter illegal financial flows.

Both countries should make the achievement of further progress in establishing robust global anti-money-laundering rules, and effective implementation, a priority of their presidencies.

At present, there is far more scrutiny of how money is made than how it is moved. And the West demands higher anti-corruption standards of its own companies overseas than it does of foreign money that flows in from abroad. This is a major gap in global economic governance. On grounds of ethics, policy consistency and security, it is time to close it.

What Needs to Happen

- A first priority in strengthening anti-money-laundering efforts is to establish a universal norm of transparent beneficial ownership of corporate vehicles.
- Public registries must ensure that beneficial owners are declared as natural persons, not legal entities. These registries should be standardized and interconnected to facilitate cooperation.
- Intermediaries need to be regulated effectively. Mandatory due diligence should include establishing the identity of beneficial owners of the entities serviced.
- Effective implementation and enforcement will require much greater resourcing. Political leaders should drive this process, including ensuring adequate funding for research.
- Western countries should take the lead in strengthening global norms, ensuring national-level compliance and developing capacity. Established best practice can provide the basis for peer assistance and technical support to other states.
- The G7 presidencies of the US and the UK, in 2020 and 2021 respectively, offer a natural opportunity to demonstrate global leadership. Both countries should use their terms to strengthen rules and implementation.

Notes

1. van der Does de Willebois, E., Halter, E. M., Harrison, R. A., Park, J. W. and Sharman, J. C. (2011), The Puppet Masters: How the Corrupt Use Legal Structures to Hide Stolen Assets and What to Do About It, Washington DC: World Bank.

2. See FACT Coalition (2019), 'FACT Sheet: Anonymous Companies and National Security (May 2019)', 17 May 2019, https://thefactcoalition.org/fact-sheet-anonymous-companies-and-national-security-may-2019; and Fuller, C. R. (2019), 'Financial transparency is not only about rule of law but also national security', American Enterprise Institute, 12 March 2019, https://www.aei.org/publication/financial-transparency-is-not-only-about-rule-of-law-but-also-national-security/.

3. For a discussion of progress towards beneficial ownership transparency, and the challenges that remain, see Adam Smith International (2019), Towards a Global Norm of Beneficial Ownership Transparency: A scoping study on a strategic approach to achieving a global norm, https://issuu.com/adamsmithinternational/docs/towards_a_global_norm_of_beneficial_9f6920e1fce9a4.

4. Sorensen, M. S. (2019), 'Estonia Orders Danske Bank Out After Money-Laundering Scandal, New York Times, 20 February 2019, https://www.nytimes.com/2019/02/20/business/danske-bank-estonia-money-laundering.html; and Danske Bank (2018), 'Findings of the investigations relating to Danske Bank's branch in Estonia', press release, 19 September 2018, https://danskebank.com/news-and-insights/news-archive/press-releases/2018/pr19092018.

14

Internal Revenue Service Law
Helps Stop Money Laundering

Internal Revenue Service

The Internal Revenue Service (IRS) is a governmental agency of the United States. It is the national tax collection organization and enacts the Internal Revenue Code authorized by Congress.

In the United States there is a law that requires any cash transactions of over $10,000 to be reported to the government. No matter who or what is conducting this transaction, federal law requires paperwork to be filed to fully account for any type of dealings that involve large amounts of cash. A variety of examples show how this reporting works and what types of businesses or personal transactions are covered under this law. It discusses the role of businesses and individuals in adhering to this law and helping to prevent money laundering.

Federal law requires a person to report cash transactions of more than $10,000 by filing IRS Form 8300, Report of Cash Payments Over $10,000 Received in a Trade or Business. The information on the form helps law enforcement combat money laundering, tax evasion, drug dealing, terrorist financing and other criminal activities.

"Cash payment report helps government combat money laundering," Internal Revenue Service, February 2019.

Who Is Covered

By law, a "person" is an individual, company, corporation, partnership, association, trust or estate. For example, dealers in jewelry, furniture, boats, aircraft or automobiles; pawnbrokers; attorneys; real estate brokers; insurance companies and travel agencies are among those who typically need to file Form 8300.

Tax-exempt organizations are also "persons" and may need to report certain transactions. A tax-exempt organization doesn't have to file Form 8300 for a charitable cash contribution. Note, however, that under a separate requirement, a donor often must obtain a written acknowledgement of the contribution from the organization. See Publication 526, Charitable Contributions, for details. But the organization must report noncharitable cash payments on Form 8300. For example, an exempt organization that receives more than $10,000 in cash for renting part of its building must report the transaction.

What's Cash

For Form 8300 reporting, cash includes coins and currency of the United States or any foreign country. It's also a cashier's check (sometimes called a treasurer's check or bank check), bank draft, traveler's check or money order with a face amount of $10,000 or less that a person receives for:

- A designated reporting transaction or
- Any transaction in which the person knows the payer is trying to avoid a report.

Note that under a separate reporting requirement, banks and other financial institutions report cash purchases of cashier's checks, treasurer's checks and/or bank checks, bank drafts, traveler's checks and money orders with a face value of more than $10,000 by filing currency transaction reports.

A designated reporting transaction is the retail sale of tangible personal property that's generally suited for personal use, expected to last at least one year and has a sales price of more than $10,000. Examples are sales of automobiles, jewelry, mobile homes and furniture.

A designated reporting transaction is also the sale of a collectible, such as a work of art, rug, antique, metal, stamp or coin. It is also the sale of travel and entertainment, if the total price of all items for the same trip or entertainment event is more than $10,000.

Reporting Cash Payments

A person must file Form 8300 if they receive cash of more than $10,000 from the same payer or agent:

- In one lump sum.
- In two or more related payments within 24 hours. For example, a 24-hour period is 11 a.m. Tuesday to 11 a.m. Wednesday.
- As part of a single transaction or two or more related transactions within 12 months.

Examples of Reporting Situations

Automobile Dealerships

- If a husband and wife purchased two cars at one time from the same dealer, and the dealer received a total of $10,200 in cash, the dealer can view the transaction as a single transaction or two related transactions. Either way, it calls for only one Form 8300.
- A dealership doesn't file Form 8300 if a customer pays with a $7,000 wire transfer and a $4,000 cashier check. A wire transfer is not cash.
- A customer purchases a car for $9,000 cash. Within 12 months, the customer pays the dealership cash of $1,500 for accessories for that car. The dealer doesn't need to file Form 8300, unless they knew or had reason to know the transactions were connected.

Taxi Company

Weekly lease payments in cash from a taxi driver to a taxi company within 12 months is considered the same transaction. The taxi company needs to file Form 8300 when the total amount exceeds $10,000. Then, if the company receives more than $10,000 cash in additional payments from the driver within 12 months, the company must file another Form 8300.

Landlords

Landlords need to file Form 8300 once they've received more than $10,000 in cash for a lease during the year. But a person not in the trade or business of managing or leasing real property, such as someone who leases their vacation home for part of the year, doesn't need to report a cash receipt of more than $10,000.

Bail-Bonding Agent

A bail-bonding agent must file Form 8300 when they receive more than $10,000 in cash from a person. This applies to payments from persons who have been arrested or anticipate arrest. The agent needs to file the form even though they haven't provided a service when they received the cash.

Colleges and Universities

Colleges and universities must file Form 8300, if they receive more than $10,000 in cash in one or more transactions within 12 months.

Home Builders

Home builders and contractors need to file Form 8300 if they receive cash of more than $10,000 for building, renovating or remodeling.

When to File Form 8300

A business must file Form 8300 within 15 days after the date the business received the cash. If a business receives later payments toward a single transaction or two or more related transactions, the business should file Form 8300 when the total amount paid exceeds $10,000.

Each time payments aggregate more than $10,000, the business must file another Form 8300.

How to File

A person can file Form 8300 electronically using the Financial Crimes Enforcement Network's BSA E-Filing System. E-filing is free, quick and secure. Filers will receive an electronic acknowledgement of each submission.

Those who prefer to mail Form 8300 can send it to Internal Revenue Service, Federal Building, P.O. Box 32621, Detroit, MI 48232. Filers can confirm the IRS received the form by sending it via certified mail with return receipt requested or calling the Detroit Federal Building at 866-270-0733.

Taxpayer Identification Number

Form 8300 requires the taxpayer identification number (TIN) of the person paying with cash. If they refuse to provide it, the business should inform the person that the IRS may assess a penalty.

If the business is unable to obtain the customer's TIN, the business should file Form 8300 anyway. The business needs to include a statement with Form 8300 that explains why the form doesn't have a TIN. The business should keep records showing it requested the customer's TIN and give the records to the IRS upon request.

Informing Customers About Form 8300 Filing

The business must give a customer written notice by Jan. 31 of the year following the transaction that it filed Form 8300 to report the customer's cash transaction.

- The government doesn't offer a specific format for the customer statement, but it must:
- Be a single statement aggregating the value of the prior year's transactions,

- Have the name, address and phone number of the person who needs to file the Form 8300 and
- Inform the customer the business is reporting the payment to the IRS.

A business can give a customer who only had one transaction during the year a copy of the invoice or Form 8300 as notification if it has the required information. The government doesn't recommend using a copy of Form 8300 because of sensitive information on the form, such as the employer identification number or Social Security number of the person filing the Form 8300.

A business may voluntarily file Form 8300 to report a suspicious transaction below $10,000. In this situation, the business doesn't let the customer know about the report. The law prohibits a business from informing a customer that it marked the suspicious transaction box on the form.

15

Time to Root Out Money Laundering in Global Trade

Andrea Durkin

Andrea Durkin has served as a US government trade negotiator and teaches international policy in the master of science in foreign service program at Georgetown University.

A huge volume of global monetary transactions occurs on a daily basis. Unfortunately, a significant percentage of this trade also involves illegal money laundering. There are many ways for criminals to fake trade transactions and thereby change illicit financial sums into legal money, and they use known schemes to achieve their goals. Is there a way to stem this flood of criminal activity? Regulations and anti-money laundering actions need to be increased, particularly in the trade of certain items and when the transactions are occurring between developing countries and advanced economies.

C HIPS is the largest private US dollar clearing system in the world. The system is used to clear and settle an average $1.67 trillion in domestic and international payments *every day*. In 2017, CHIPS handled $393.2 trillion in payments.

In comparison, all of the merchandise trade transacted in the world in 2017 amounted to $17.73 trillion, according to the World Trade Organization. Another $5.28 trillion in commercial services were traded. As a small fraction of bank business, monitoring

"How Criminals Move Money Through Global Trade," by Andrea Durkin, TradeVistas, May 17, 2019. Reprinted by permission.

payments to spot "trade-based money laundering" has been a lesser priority for private banks within the larger world of financial crime prevention.

But as global trade grows and increases in complexity, trade-based money laundering has become the weakest link in anti-money laundering initiatives, so banks and government officials are strengthening international collaboration to crack down on criminals who hide and launder their dirty money in global trade transactions.

False Invoicing and Other Shenanigans

As the Economist wrote a few years ago, "cuddly toys don't have to be stuffed with cocaine or cash to be useful to traffickers." Instead, a drug trafficking organization in California can buy toys from China with dirty money, re-export them to their home country in South America, and sell the toys in exchange for local pesos, effectively washing their drug money (a real example).

These kinds of normal-looking transactions enable transnational criminals to disguise billions in proceeds from their crimes, moving the money across borders and intermingling it into the formal economy through trade. How do they do it? They falsify trade documents, misrepresent trade-related financial transactions, or both.

Among the most common schemes are over-invoicing and under-invoicing commodities whereby the shipper, often colluding with the importer, misrepresents the price of goods. The difference between the declared value of the goods and money paid in the transaction represents illicit money exchanging hands undetected. In other cases, a shipper invoices the same shipment multiple times, receiving payment over and over for one shipment. In more brazen cases of "phantom shipping," a fake invoice travels alone with no merchandise associated with it.

Criminals can even co-opt an unwitting legitimate business. An unsuspecting company might receive an online order, invoice and ship the goods to a business in country A, but the payment is made by some separate third-party in country B.

Red Flags: Cigarettes, Gems, and… Home Appliances?

The volume, complexities, and speed of global trade transactions make finding these illegitimate schemes challenging for law enforcement and financial institutions.

Authorities and payment institutions scan for indicators of funny business, such as payments made to vendors by unrelated third parties in the example above. They report incidents of document falsification, creating databases for use by customs officials. They look for mismatches between commodities traded and types of businesses involved, unusual shipping routes or transshipment points, and double invoicing.

Banks also look for unusual customer behaviors and transaction structures. Authorities are on high alert when reviewing trade in "high-risk commodities" such as gems and precious metals, tobacco products, and even consumer electronics and home appliances. They work to identify global "hotspots" with higher incidence of trade-based money laundering and monitor for shipments involving those countries.

According to a 2010 Treasury Department advisory notice to financial institutions, transactions involving entities in Mexico and China were the most frequently named in "suspicious activity reports" (SARs) produced by US law enforcement regarding possible trade-based money laundering. The advisory noted that SARs involving transactions in China continued to increase while those citing a connection to Mexico were beginning to decrease. That same advisory report identified rapid growth in potential trade-based money laundering activities involving Venezuela.

Following the Money

In the game of money laundering, the trade transaction provides the vehicle and cover for some form of payment.

Trade financing to support those payments include a suite of services such as bank guarantees, document collection, import/export loans, pre-shipment loans, trust receipts, warehouse financing, and structured trade financing. Through organizations like the Bankers Association for Finance and Trade (BAFT), financial institutions have common guidance on red flags and ways to comply with "know your customer" legal requirements for trade finance transactions.

But banks only have adequate visibility into trade transactions that require documentation on the underlying transaction. In a "documentary" transaction, the bank handles paperwork such as bills of lading, invoices, packing lists, certificates of origin and other forms of underlying information surrounding the transaction. In this scenario, banks can monitor and review for any red flags before executing payment.

The problem is that at least 80 percent of trade is "open account," according to BAFT. In facilitating these payments, banks might provide pre-shipment financing, without information about the nature of the shipment itself. Or the bank might clear a single net payment via wire transfer, settling multiple transactions among parties without any paperwork on the nature of the underlying trade transactions themselves.

Customs Authorities as a Line of Defense

Because banks often lack sufficient documentation to prevent trade-based money laundering, the task of catching the criminals still falls mainly to customs authorities who have access to more detailed manifests and declarations provided by shippers. Portions of the full data set they need, however, are collected by different entities.

Some pieces of the puzzle are gathered directly by federal customs and some by port authorities. Other important information remains in the private sector with banks, insurers, brokers, storage services, and logistics companies. Having greater ability to pool that data while respecting business confidentiality would offer authorities a better chance to create big trade data they could then marry with other contextual information like crime statistics and satellite imagery to improve their ability to spot patterns or irregularities.

As well, customs agencies are working to enhance cooperation across national jurisdictions to get a full line of sight, comparing official import records with official export records for significant mismatches. Without such collaboration, customs agencies can't see both sides of a trade transaction where discrepancies can occur.

Customs compliance officers face another significant hurdle in determining accurate and reasonable pricing for commodities. How much should a particular cell phone cost: $200, $450, $850? What about a dress, or jewelry of varying quality?

Homeland Security established a Trade Transparency Unit in 2004 which piloted a special computer system called the Data Analysis and Research for Trade Transparency System (DARTT). DARTT aggregates data across all shipments to detect and analyze price variations that fall outside a range, allowing customs to sharpen the focus of its transaction reviews. Better global data collection in digital form and the deployment of secure data sharing mechanisms will help customs agencies combat money laundering in global trade, but most customs officials around the world still operate in a low-tech environment. The US government has been working to help other governments stand up units like the US Trade Transparency Unit, mainly throughout Latin America.

A "Persistent" Feature in North-South Trade

Global Financial Integrity is an organization that estimates the volume of illicit flows into and out of 148 developing and emerging countries that piggyback onto trade in goods with advanced economies. They believe trade-based money laundering and cheating by falsifying trade documents is a "significant and persistent feature" of developing country trade with advanced economies. Their latest annual report suggests it is a particular problem in outflows from resource-rich countries such as South

Africa and Nigeria, but detected in every region. GFI says that over the last ten years, as much as 48 percent of Mozambique's trade with advanced economics is illicit, as is 44 percent of Malawi's trade, 43 percent of Zambia's, 39.7 percent of Honduras, and 30.8 percent of Myanmar's trade with advanced economies.

Inflating values on customs documents can allow exporters to skirt capital controls by moving more money out of a country that would otherwise be allowed; under-invoicing can be used by importers to evade taxes and duties. Governments lose revenue and undervalued goods enter the marketplace, undermining fair competition for legitimate businesses. Illicit inflows often fuel further illegal activities in the receiving country.

Given the persistence and growing nature of trade-based money laundering, both government-to-government collaboration and the deployment of innovative technologies to analyze big data and predict illicit behaviors will be key ingredients to staying ahead of this trend and enabling unimpeded growth of legitimate businesses engaging in global trade.

16

Anti–Money Laundering Policies Unintentionally Punish Poor Countries

Clay Lowery and Vijaya Ramachandran

Clay Lowery is a nonresident fellow at the Center for Global Development and Vijaya Ramachandran is senior fellow at the Center for Global Development.

Countries around the world recognize the negative consequences that money laundering poses. In response, governments and leaders have taken drastic steps to combat money laundering. Unfortunately, some of these new strict policies are actually proving problematic for countries trying to alleviate poverty. Some of those who are negatively impacted by these policies include migrants trying to send money home, vulnerable individuals in post-disaster or conflict situations, and small firms in poor countries. However, there are ways to improve financial security without making poor countries pay the price.

Money laundering, terrorism financing and sanctions violations by individuals, banks and other financial entities are serious offenses with significant negative consequences for rich and poor countries alike. Governments have taken important steps to address these offenses. Efforts by international organizations, the US, UK and others to combat money laundering and curb illicit financial flows are a necessary step to increase the safety of

"Unintended Consequences of Anti–Money Laundering Policies for Poor Countries," by Clay Lowery and Vijaya Ramachandran, Center for Global Development, November 9, 2015. Reprinted by permission.

the financial system and improve security, both domestically and around the world. But the policies that have been put in place to counter financial crimes may also have unintentional and costly consequences, in particular for people in poor countries.[1] Those most affected are likely to include the families of migrant workers, small businesses that need to access working capital or trade finance, and recipients of life-saving aid in active-conflict, post-conflict or post-disaster situations. And sometimes, current policies may be self-defeating to the extent that they reduce the transparency of financial flows.

Under the current approach, banks are asked to prevent sanctions violations and assess and mitigate money laundering (ML) and terrorist financing (TF) risks, or face penalties. However, regulators sometimes send mixed signals about whether and how banks and other entities should manage their ML/TF risk, which sometimes results in simplistic risk assessment methodologies being applied by these entities. There may also be a chilling effect resulting from the imposition of legitimate fines on some large banks for egregious contraventions of anti-money laundering, counter the financing of terror and, particularly, sanctions laws (commonly referred to collectively as AML/CFT). These factors, along with others, have led banks to adopt an understandably conservative position. This includes exiting from providing services to firms, market segments and countries that are seen as higher risk, lower profitability and could become the source of costly future fines, monitorships or even prosecutions. Banks are engaging in "de-risking" by ceasing to engage in types of activities that are seen to be higher risk in a wholesale fashion, rather than judging the risks of clients on a case-by-case basis.[2]

Individual banks may be acting rationally in not serving certain types of clients, due to a variety of factors. However, the implementation of AML/CFT appears to have created categories of clients whose business cannot justify the associated compliance costs. The financial exclusion of such clients creates yet another obstacle for poverty alleviation and economic growth, especially in poor countries. While the consequences seem manifold, the data are too weak to make systemic judgments. That said, we do observe some correlations between AML/CFT policies and debanking of money transfer organizations, correspondent banking, and non-profits trying to access banking services in difficult environments:

- Migrants who want to send money home and the families who rely on that money need a healthy money transfer organization (MTO) sector. These MTOs are seeing banking services denied, downgraded, or made more expensive. In other words, MTOs are pushed out of one bank and have to find another that may be more expensive, or based in a less transparent jurisdiction. In 2013, more than 140 UK-based remittance companies were told by Barclays Bank that their accounts would be closed. Following this, and similar de-banking episodes in the US and Australia, only larger money transfer organizations have access to bank accounts. Industry bodies report that many smaller players have been forced to close, become agents of larger businesses, or even disguise the true nature of their operations in order to remain banked. Given that remittances from migrant workers total $440bn a year (more than three times foreign aid), a vital source of finance for poor countries might be affected.

- Vulnerable people in post-disaster or conflict situations rely on non-profit organizations (NPOs) to deliver humanitarian assistance. Citizens of all countries rely on NPOs to assist in sustainably reducing the incidence of terrorism. But these same (NPOs) report difficulties carrying out operations. For instance, HSBC closed the bank account of several NPOs including the Cordoba Foundation, a think tank that receives money from the UK government for work to prevent terrorism, saying only that continuing to bank the organization «fell outside the bank's risk appetite."

- Small to medium-sized firms in poor countries lack the credit they need to create jobs. To get access to this credit, they need local banks to have easy connections to large international banks. Unfortunately, rich country banks increasingly report withdrawing correspondent banking services from banks in high risk jurisdictions, including many poor countries, reducing their access to the global financial system.

- Regulators may also be losing out. They find it more difficult to track transactions as MTOs who cannot send funds electronically begin to use potentially less transparent mechanisms including bulk currency exchanges, and as banks and businesses in poor countries have to send funds via banks with less robust compliance programs and operating in less transparent jurisdictions instead of directly to rich countries. In the long term, this threatens public safety and economic stability across the globe.

So serious is the problem of de-risking that Mark Carney, Governor of the Bank of England and Chairman of the Financial Stability Board, has termed it "financial abandonment," while Janet Yellen, Chair of the US Federal Reserve, acknowledged before Congress that rich countries' AML/CFT rules were "causing a great deal of hardship." In 2015, the G20 Finance Ministers and Central Bank Governors welcomed work by the FSB that addresses the withdrawal of correspondent banking.

In this report we catalogue extensive suggestive evidence of some of the unintended consequences of AML/CFT and sanctions enforcement. We recognize that FATF and others are already taking steps to address these problems and we welcome their efforts. In this report, we recommend five key actions that should be taken by public officials—particularly in the Financial Action Task Force (FATF, the global standard setting body for AML/CFT) and the Financial Stability Board (FSB, which coordinates and reviews the work of the international standard setting bodies)—as well as by national regulators, banks, MTOs and NPOs. The support of the United States, the United Kingdom and other rich countries for these efforts are critical, as is that of the G20.

National regulators should work to reduce regulatory uncertainty and provide clear signals to banks and other financial institutions. Banks should also play a role, especially by continuing to invest in portable identity verification and tracking. Money transfer organizations and non-profits should make greater efforts to implement and demonstrate effective compliance systems. Better cooperation among regulators, policy makers, and private actors would enable meeting the twin goals of stopping money going to bad actors and allowing finance to flow in an efficient and transparent way.

Where necessary, the actions we recommend need to be taken in conjunction with other specialist organizations such as the United Nations and the EU (sanctions), the Basel Committee on Banking Supervision (standard setter for bank supervision), the Committee on Payments and Market Infrastructures (standard setter for payment systems), the IMF and the World Bank. The Financial Action Task Force (FATF) is the global standard-setting body for AML/CFT. However, it has stated, in line with the evidence, that de-risking behavior has many drivers, a number of which lie outside its mandate. A process led by the FSB and supported by FATF is appropriate.[3]

We summarize five recommendations below. While some of the following recommendations are potentially "quick wins" that could be enacted rapidly and at little cost, others would take several years to implement and will require significant financing, both from governments and from the private sector.

Seriously Assess the Unintended Consequences of AML/CFT and Sanctions Enforcement at the National and the Global Level

The strength of the suggestive evidence detailed in this report requires a rigorous causal investigation of the unintended consequences of AML/CFT enforcement.

- The FSB should conduct a rigorous assessment of the global AML/CFT and sanctions regulatory environment, including the guidance produced by FATF, with a view to reducing unintended consequences.

- FATF should continue to enhance its mutual evaluation methodology to include:
  - Displacement of transactions from more into less transparent channels, which are sometimes informal or processed through lower-tier, less compliant institutions
  - Risks in the whole economy, rather than just in the formal financial sector
  - Risks posed to the important drive toward financial inclusion
  - Over-compliance at the national level and in particular sectors

Generate Better Data and Share Data

In order to assess unintended consequences rigorously, more and better data should be generated through private and public sector efforts.

- The World Bank should make publicly available, both the results and if possible, the underlying anonymized data, from its de-risking survey of banks, MTOs and governments as soon as possible.
- The FSB should direct the World Bank to carry out representative, countrywide surveying of NPOs involved in the delivery of humanitarian assistance, banks and MTOs.
- Government agencies that keep detailed registries of regulated MTOs and NPOs should make available headline statistics about the numbers and nature of such organizations.
- National financial intelligence units, including but not limited to FinCEN, should query financial institutions for data regarding the volume, amounts and types of transactions associated with MTOs, NPOs and banking correspondents.

- On behalf of central banks and private financial institutions; SWIFT, CHIPS, CHAPS, BIS and other entities tasked with managing and collecting data on cross-border transactions and relationships should make available data on bilateral payment flows and the number of correspondent banking relationships between countries.
- National governments should make the data that they are using for risk analyses and regulatory impact assessments available to other jurisdictions and to parties conducting analyses that are demonstrably in the public interest.

Strengthen the Risk-Based Approach

FATF should be congratulated for introducing and recently strengthening its risk-based approach. However, it needs to be applied more extensively and more consistently.

- FATF should provide a definition of money laundering and terrorist financing risk for its purposes that is consistent with a standardized definition (as provided by the International Organization for Standardization) and existing private sector definitions of "risk."

- FATF should clarify its thinking regarding transparency and the tradeoff of risk in the formal versus informal sector.

- FATF should further encourage simplified due diligence where it is in the best interests of transparency.

- FATF should urgently revise Recommendation 8 to reflect the fact that NPOs may be vulnerable to terrorist abuse by virtue of their activities, rather than whether they happen to be an NPO or not.

Improve Compliance and Clarify
Indicators of Lower Risk

Compliance procedures at many NPOs and MTOs must be improved so as to be more effective. At the same time, more needs to be done to recognize those NPOs and MTOs that do have effective systems in place, including better supervision of MTO sectors at the country level.

- Many NPOs and MTOs, especially smaller ones, should improve their compliance procedures to ensure money laundering and terrorist financing risks are mitigated effectively and efficiently.
- FATF should provide greater clarity on the likely indicators of lower risk NPOs and MTOs, and national governments and industry participants should collaborate to reflect this guidance with best practice documents.

Facilitate Identification and Lower the Costs of Compliance

National governments, banks and the World Bank should accelerate the adoption of new and existing technology to facilitate lower cost customer identification, know your customer compliance, and due diligence.

- National governments should provide citizens with the means to identify themselves in order to make reliably identifying clients possible for financial institutions and other organizations.
- National governments should ensure that appropriate privacy frameworks and accountability measures support these identification efforts while ensuring the free flow of information related to identifying ML and TF.
- Banks and other financial institutions should redouble their efforts, with encouragement from the FSB and national regulators, to develop and adopt better messaging standards and implement KYC documentation repositories.
- Banks and other financial institutions should accelerate the global adoption of the Legal Entity Identifier scheme.
- The World Bank should convene all relevant entities to review the possibility of donor-subsidized third party verification for unprofitable clients.

Notes

1. We use the term "poor countries" to describe the countries that the World Bank classifies as "low-income economies" and "lower middle-income economies." These are countries with GNI per capita of less than $4,125.

2. "De-risking" is sometimes used in this way, and sometimes in a more general sense, to refer broadly to the process of reducing exposure to risk. We employ the more restrictive definition of "de-risking" for clarity, in order to avoid confusion between "good" and "bad" de-risking.

3. The FSB's mandate includes a responsibility to "undertake joint strategic reviews of the policy development work of the [financial regulatory] international standard setting bodies to ensure their work is timely, coordinated, focused on priorities, and addressing gaps" as well as to "assess vulnerabilities affecting the financial system and identify and oversee action needed to address them" and "advise on and monitor best practice in meeting regulatory standards." For full detail, see FSB. "Mandate," accessed 22 October, 2015.

17

Global Anti–Money Laundering Efforts Fail to Stop Crime

Ronald F. Pol

Ronald F. Pol is a researcher at the New Zealand Law Society and a senior researcher at La Trobe University.

Despite the number of high-profile money laundering busts that are reported on in the news, the vast majority of money laundering schemes go uncaught. In fact, according to estimates from the UN, only 0.1 to 0.2 percent of criminal assets are ever seized. Although reforms were made in 2014 to the global anti-money laundering system and efforts to stop money laundering have increased since then, the proportion of money launderers who are caught has not gone up. What these reforms have resulted in are complicated laws, too many regulators, and costly compliance practices.

Money laundering rarely gets as literal as the case in Thailand last week, where police raided homes of a ring suspected of laundering a billion baht (about A\$48 million) of drug proceeds and found millions stashed in a washing machine.

Stories about money laundering, and efforts to prevent it, are rife.

In just the past week there were reports about Swiss bank UBS agreeing to pay a €10 million (about A\$16 million) penalty to end an Italian money laundering case; a New Zealand company, Jin Yuan Finance, being fined NZ$4 million (about A$3.7 million) for not complying with anti-money laundering laws; and calls in Australia for a royal commission after leaked CCTV footage from Melbourne's Crown Casino showed a man in a tracksuit exchanging "bricks of cash" worth hundreds of thousands of dollars for gaming chips in one of the casino's high-roller rooms.

In the latter case, Crown Casino defended itself on the basis of having a "comprehensive" Anti-Money Laundering and Counter-Terrorism Financing program overseen by the Australian Transaction Reports and Analysis Centre (AUSTRAC). But federal parliamentarian Andrew Wilkie called the situation a catastrophic "multinational, multi-jurisdictional and multi-agency" failure by politicians, state regulators, police and AUSTRAC.

He's right, at least in part.

The deeper problem isn't that national anti-money laundering laws are being flouted. It's that the global anti-money laundering system is a failed experiment.

We need to have an honest conversation about what's wrong with it, including the possibility that much of it is a waste of time, and some of it might be doing more harm than good.

99% Design Failure

Don't get me wrong: money laundering controls do good things too. Suspicious transactions trigger alerts, offenders are arrested and assets seized.

But the amount of criminal funds intercepted is scarcely a drop in the bucket. The system is designed to catch *some* criminals. It has almost no impact on crime.

The United Nations Office of Drugs and Crime has estimated that just 0.2% of the proceeds of crime are seized. My update of the UN's estimate (in research not yet published) suggests the figure might now be 0.1% or less. Either way, in practical terms the "success rate" of money laundering controls is scarcely an accounting rounding error in criminal accounts.

There are many reasons for anti-money laundering's failure, but a big problem is the emphasis on activity and effort rather than results. It's the same mindset that focuses on the number of hours spent at work rather than what's achieved, or how many speeding tickets are issued instead of whether harm from accidents is reduced.

Reforms to the global anti-money laundering system, rolled out from 2014, were meant to address this problem. They didn't. Though the language of "outcomes" and "effectiveness" was used, it meant something different to the *impact* and *effect* of regulations on reducing crime and its harms.

In other words, the new measures were mislabelled "outcomes." They continued to measure effort and activity, such as the number of money laundering prosecutions, instead of the impact (if any) on crime.

Frenetic Activity

Frenetic compliance activity helps obscure the harsh reality of poor results. Casinos and banks conform to complex rules designed like a giant stack of colanders to catch water, continually adding new ones to "fix gaps." New "compliance solutions" doggedly rake over the same ground covered by those that catch less than 1% of transactions.

The upshot is that companies can show they comply with anti-money laundering laws (Crown's response is straight out of the compliance textbook) and countries can show they comply with international standards.

But does it stop crime? Who knows? The system isn't designed to demonstrate its impact on crime. Jin Yuan Finance, for example, was fined because it breached anti-money laundering laws, not because there was necessarily laundering or any other crime.

A criminal mastermind given the chance to rewrite anti-money laundering rules might just keep what we have, on the basis it keeps the authorities ineffectually busy.

Good Intentions and "Voluntary Coercion"

The problems with the system can be traced to the rushed and flawed way it was set up.

The modern anti-money laundering experiment started in 1989, at a G7 summit in Paris. The seven big industrialised nations bypassed treaty-based consensus to establish a "Financial Action Task Force" to help prevent drug trafficking. The task force—known as FATF—later targeted money laundering associated with other profit-motivated crimes and terrorism financing.

After a sluggish start, with few nations signing up to its compliance model, FATF made an offer governments couldn't refuse — ironically echoing a famous line from The Godfather.

FATF rated countries' anti-money laundering regimes and issued "black lists" and "grey lists" publicly naming those not meeting its "recommendations." Banks did the rest. Treating the ratings and lists as a proxy for risk, access to the financial system became difficult for many countries. FATF's intention (in its own words) was to "pressure" countries to comply, "to maintain their position in the global economy."

Risking exclusion from financial markets, 205 countries and jurisdictions "voluntarily" joined the anti-money laundering movement. The system depends on a set of self-declared "best-practice" standards. This means each national anti-money laundering regime reflects the flaws of the international standard.

At the UN General Assembly last month, leaders from small and large countries railed against the perceived unfairness and damage caused by blacklists and financial sanctions.

Such protests might be more easily dismissed as self-serving if the anti-money laundering system worked. But it doesn't.

Complicated laws, armies of regulators and costly compliance tasks give the comfort of activity and feeling of security, but they don't make us safe from serious crime and terrorism. To resolve it, we must frankly confront the reality of its failure.

18

Effective Anti–Money Laundering Procedures Must Be Enforced and Scrutinized

Sean Curley

Sean Curley is dean of the School of Law, Policing and Forensics at Staffordshire University in the United Kingdom.

This viewpoint examines the case of Danske Bank, a Danish bank that facilitated the laundering of billions of euros in its Estonian branch between 2007 and 2015. According to the author, this scenario brings into question whether banks and governments are equipped to combat money laundering. Though Danske had their own anti-money laundering procedures in place, they were ineffective at preventing suspicious transactions from occurring. Curley asserts that criminal sanctions for noncompliance with anti money laundering procedures and increased scrutiny of how guidelines are implemented are necessary to more effectively combat money laundering.

I t is clear that Danske Bank has failed to live up to its responsibility in the case of possible money laundering in Estonia." So said Thomas Borgen, CEO of Denmark's biggest financial institution, when he resigned after admitting that around €200 billion of questionable money flowed through the Danish bank's Estonian branch from 2007-15.

"Danske Bank: the story of Europe's biggest money laundering scandal," by Sean Curley, The Conversation, October 22, 2018, https://theconversation.com/danske-bank-the-story-of-europes-biggest-money-laundering-scandal-104865. Licensed under CC BY-ND 4.0 International.

To put that figure into some perspective, the GDP of Estonia in 2017 was €29 billion and the figure in question is approaching two thirds of the GDP of Denmark itself at €324 billion.

It raises serious questions over the capacity of banks—and governments—to combat the serious scourge of money laundering. The European Commission has called the case the "biggest scandal in Europe" and Danske Bank and Denmark and Estonia's financial watchdogs face an inquiry from the European Union's banking supervisor to see whether they broke the law.

Money laundering facilitates crime, undermines financial systems and ultimately can seriously damage economies. This is all well recognised—and yet it seems that even the world's most sophisticated financial regimes cannot control the flow of suspect money through the system.

To get some perspective on the scale of the problem, the National Crime Agency estimates that the cost of money laundering to the UK economy is £24 billion a year. Globally, it is estimated that up to 5% of global GDP—that's £1.5 trillion—is laundered by criminals each year.

Money laundering is the process by which "dirty money"—which is to say money that is identifiable as the proceeds of crime—is made to look legitimate by passing it through financial systems to disguise its suspicious origins.

Various techniques are used, generally involving layers of transactions. This may involve moving money through different countries and then returning it in a way that looks legitimate. It may involve spurious transactions at inflated values such as paying a high price for a shell company, the purchase and resale of property or legitimate businesses.

Even fake litigation has been used to disguise the ultimate source of funds—a cash intensive business is set up, documents are created to suggest a legitimate debt and then a solicitor is approached to recover it. When the fake debtor makes a payment, the funds are passed through the solicitor's bank account and back to the client.

The Danske Case

In recognition of the extent of the problem, the G7 group of major economies formed the Financial Action Task Force on Money Laundering back in 1989. The idea behind this was to produce a set of standards and guidelines and to monitor progress on anti-money laundering regimes.

The focus is to identify suspicious transactions and report them. For anti-money laundering efforts to be successful, it requires financial institutions to know their customers. This means that banks must be able to identify the ultimate beneficial recipient of a transaction—so the person who takes the profit—of any customer on their books.

This is where Danske Bank ran into trouble. Its Estonian branch came about when Danske acquired Sampo Bank, a small Finnish Bank in 2007. Sampo had a non-resident portfolio in Estonia and it is this that caused the problems.

In the words of the independent report into the scandal, which preempted CEO Borgen's resignation: "Anti-money laundering procedures at the Estonian branch had been manifestly insufficient and inadequate." Danske Bank has also admitted there were "major deficiencies in controls and governance that made it possible to use Danske Bank's branch in Estonia for criminal activities such as money laundering."

Danske shut down the non-resident portfolio in 2015 after it became clear that the bank's anti-money laundering procedures at the Estonian branch weren't working. As a mere branch, Estonia should have been subject to Danske's own money laundering systems—but the branch had its own IT platform, which meant it was not covered by the same risk monitoring as the bank's Copenhagen headquarters.

The independent investigation found that more than half of Danske's 15,000 customers in Estonia were suspicious. The source of funds passing through the portfolio was identified as more than 58% coming from Russia, Estonia and Latvia. The destinations of the funds were worldwide.

The difficulty in identifying the true source of the funds comes from the lack of transparency as to the real owners of the customers in the portfolio. A proportion of them are UK-based companies that are registered as limited liability partnerships—this means they are not required to publish details of their eventual owners. This is a classic case of money laundering where ownership often passes through a series of shell companies before the eventual owner can be identified.

The customers are being investigated by several national authorities including the FBI and the UK National Crime Agency. The Danish regulator is investigating Danske Bank itself. Harsh penalties for the bank could ensue—Denmark's business minister said the Danish authorities could fine Danske 4 billion Danish kroner (£475m). But it remains to be seen what the long-term damage will be for Danske, if any.

A wider question surrounds the failure of international anti-money laundering regimes. To date there have been no examples of significant criminal sanctions for failure to implement an effective anti-money laundering process within a business. Nor is there any rigorous external scrutiny of how guidelines are implemented. But it is high time there was—while there is still a financial system to protect.

Organizations to Contact

The editors have compiled the following list of organizations concerned with the issues debated in this book. The descriptions are derived from materials provided by the organizations. All have publications or information available for interested readers. The list was compiled on the date of publication of the present volume; the information provided here may change. Be aware that many organizations take several weeks or longer to respond to inquiries, so allow as much time as possible.

The Brookings Institution
1775 Massachusetts Avenue NW
Washington, DC 20036
phone: (202) 797-6000
website: www.brookings.edu

The Brookings Institution is a nonprofit public policy organization focused on research and problem-solving for the good of society. Their experts from all over the world report on important issues—including money laundering—that can be consumed through articles, blog posts, books, and more.

The Carnegie Council
170 East 64th Street
New York, NY 10065
phone: (212) 838-4120
email: info@cceia.org
website: www.carnegiecouncil.org

The Carnegie Council for Ethics in International Affairs is a nonpartisan agency dedicated to inspiring and guiding debate and educating the public about issues related to ethics on the global stage. Their website offers articles, podcasts, the organization's journal *Ethics and International Affairs*.

Council on Foreign Relations (CFR)
58 East 68th Street
New York, NY 10065
phone: (212) 434-9400
website: www.cfr.org

The Council on Foreign Relations is an independent, nonpartisan organization and think tank dedicated to providing informational resources to those interested in understanding the world and the international policy issues affecting the United States. The CFR maintains a website with information geared at world issues on a variety of topics.

Federal Bureau of Investigation (FBI)
935 Pennsylvania Avenue NW
Washington, DC 20535-0001
phone: (202) 234-3000
website: www.fbi.gov

The Federal Bureau of Investigation is a crime-fighting agency of the United States government. The agency's main mission is to protect the people of the United States and uphold the US Constitution. The FBI maintains a comprehensive site providing information in a number of formats—articles, videos, podcasts, radio, photos and more—about all types of crimes, including money laundering.

Federal Reserve System
20th Street and Constitution Avenue NW
Washington, DC 20551
phone: (202) 452-3000
website: www.federalreserve.gov

The Federal Reserve System is the central bank of the United States. It aims to provide US citizens with a safe, stable monetary and banking system. Individuals can learn all about the financial systems of the US through articles, videos, and publications.

Financial Crimes Enforcement Network (FinCEN)
PO Box 39
Vienna, VA 22183
phone: (800) 767-2825
email: FRC@fincen.gov
website: www.fincen.gov

The Financial Crimes Enforcement Network is a US governmental bureau within the Department of the Treasury. Its main mission is to safeguard the US financial system and to combat money laundering. This site contains information about the history of anti-money laundering laws.

Foundation for Defense of Democracies (FDD)
PO Box 33249
Washington, DC 20033
phone: (202) 207-0190
email: info@fdd.org
website: www.fdd.org

The Foundation for Defense of Democracies is a nonpartisan organization based in Washington, DC. The FDD focuses its efforts on strengthening the national security of the United States and performs research aimed at this objective. Their website contains articles on international topics including money laundering and other illegal financial issues.

Institute for Policy Studies (IPS)
1301 Connecticut Avenue NW
Washington, DC 20036
phone: (202) 234-9382
email: info@ips-dc.org
website: www.ips-dc.org

The Institute for Policy Studies is a think tank dedicated to a peaceful society that is ecologically sustainable and socially equitable. Read about current news topics, including those of economic interest.

The Organization for Economic Co-operation and Development (OECD)

OECD Washington Center
1776 I Street NW, Suite 450
Washington, DC 20006
phone: (202) 785-6323
email: washington.contact@oecd.org
website: www.oecd.org/unitedstates/

The Organization for Economic Co-operation and Development is an international group that seeks to enhance trade relations and economic development between partner members. Member countries are limited to democracies with a market economy. Their current goals include shaping policies that promote economic growth while considering equality and opportunity for citizens.

US Department of the Treasury

1500 Pennsylvania Avenue NW
Washington, DC 20220
phone: (202) 622-2000
website: https://home.treasury.gov/

The US Department of the Treasury is a governmental department of the United States. The website maintained by the agency provides a vast array of information, including on issues of financial concern.

US Drug Enforcement Agency (DEA)

800 K Street NW
Suite 500
Washington, DC 20001
phone: (202) 305-8500
website: www.dea.gov

The US Drug Enforcement Agency is an agency of the US government. The agency maintains a robust site with many types of resources connected to the issues of drugs and drug enforcement, which includes money laundering.

US Securities and Exchange Commission (SEC)
100 F Street NE
Washington, DC 20549
website: www.sec.gov

The US Securities and Exchange Commission is a governmental agency that protects US securities markets and those who invest in these markets. The SEC aims to provide information to all interested investors, whether they are individuals investing small amounts of money or large businesses in the financial sector of the US economy.

Bibliography

Books

Dean C. Alexander. *Business Confronts Terrorism: Risks and Responses.* Madison, WI: University of Wisconsin Press, 2004.

Erin Arvudland. *Open Secret: The Global Banking Conspiracy that Swindled Investors out of Billions.* New York, NY: Penguin, 2014.

Jake Bernstein. *Secrecy World: Inside the Panama Papers Investigation of Illicit Money Networks and the Global Elite.* New York, NY: Henry Holt & Company, 2017.

Oliver Bullough. *Moneyland: The Inside Story of the Crooks and Kleptocrats Who Rule the World.* New York, NY: St. Martin's Press, 2019.

John A. Cassara. *Hide & Seek: Intelligence, Law Enforcement, and the Stalled War on Terrorist Finance.* Washington, DC: Potomac Books, 2006.

Ian DeMartino. *The Bitcoin Guidebook: How to Obtain, Invest, and Spend the World's First Decentralized Cryptocurrency.* New York, NY: Skyhorse Publishing, 2019.

Benton E. Gup. *Money Laundering, Financing Terrorism and Suspicious Activities.* Hauppauge, NY: Nova Science Publishers, 2007.

Brian Kelly. *Bitcoin Big Bank: How Alternative Currencies Are About to Change the World.* Hoboken, NY: John Wiley & Sons, 2015.

Arvind Narayanan. *Bitcoin and Cryptocurrency Technologies: A Comprehensive Introduction.* Princeton, NJ: Princeton University Press, 2016.

Peter Reuter. *Chasing Dirty Money: The Fight Against Money Laundering.* Washington, DC: Institute for International Economics, 2004.

Kannan Subramanian. *The Money Laundering & Financing of Terrorism Eco-System.* Chennai, India: Notion Press, 2016.

Paul Vigna. *The Age of Cryptocurrency: How Bitcoin and Digital Money are Challenging the Global Economic Order.* New York, NY: St. Martin's Press, 2015.

Periodicals and Internet Sources

Catherine Austin-Fitts, "Narco-Dollars for Beginners: How the Money Works in the Illicit Drug Trade," Daily Coin, January 10, 2018, https://thedailycoin.org/2018/01/10/narco-dollars-beginners-money-works-illicit-drug-trade/.

James Chen, "What is Money Laundering?" Investopedia, June 25, 2019, https://www.investopedia.com/terms/m/moneylaundering.asp.

Toby Dershowitz, "Iran's New Anti-Money Laundering Law Actually Legalizes Money Laundering," Foundation for Defense of Democracies, February 15, 2019, https://www.fdd.org/analysis/2019/02/15/irans-new-anti-money-laundering-law-actually-legalizes-money-laundering/.

Zach Dorfman, "The Ayatollah's Billion-Dollar Alaskan Bag Man," Politico, July 14, 2017, https://www.politico.com/magazine/story/2017/07/14/iran-money-laundering-kenneth-zong-215372.

Antonia Noori Farzan, "He Was the Go-To Expert on Money Laundering. Now He's Been Charged With Money Laundering," *Washington Post,* November 19, 2019, https://www.washingtonpost.com/nation/2019/11/19/bruce-bagley-money-laundering-university-miami-expert/.

Tamasin Ford, "Ivory Coast Cracks Down on Cyber Crime," BBC News, January 16, 2014, https://www.bbc.com/news/business-25735305.

Noah Friedman and Alana Kakoyiannis, "How the Super-Wealthy Hide Billions Using Tax Havens and Shell Companies," Business Insider, September 17, 2019, https://www.businessinsider.com/jake-bernstein-panama-papers-offshore-banking-shell-companies-2018-2.

Brian Mahany, "Money Laundering, Drug Trafficking & Whistleblower Awards," Mahany Law, February 9, 2018, https://www.mahanyertl.com/2018/money-laundering-whistleblower-awards/.

Cristina Maza, "Trump Made Millions of Dollars From Drug Money Laundering in Panama: Report," *Newsweek*, November 17, 2017, https://www.newsweek.com/trump-drugs-corruption-panama-hotel-money-laundering-714891.

Linda McGlasson, "Money Laundering at the Heart of NY/NJ Arrests," Bank Info Security, July 24, 2009, https://www.bankinfosecurity.com/money-laundering-at-heart-nynj-arrests-a-1652.

Melodie Michel, "Trade Based Money-Laundering: Not Just a Bank's Burden," *Global Trade Review*, May 15, 2017, https://www.gtreview.com/news/americas/trade-based-money-laundering-not-just-banks-burden/.

Anastasia Nesvetailova, "Why Russia's 'Dirty Money' is Not Leaving London Any Time Soon," Conversation, May 22, 2018, https://theconversation.com/why-russias-dirty-money-is-not-leaving-london-any-time-soon-96952.

Sammy Parks, "Houston Man Sentenced for Federal Drug Trafficking and Money Laundering Violations," US Drug Enforcement Administration, May 17, 2019, https://

www.dea.gov/press-releases/2019/05/17/houston-man-sentenced-federal-drug-trafficking-and-money-laundering.

Vanessa Romo, "US Arrests Money-Laundering Expert for Laundering Money," NPR, November 19, 2019, https://www.npr.org/2019/11/19/780877837/u-s-arrests-money-laundering-expert-for-laundering-money.

Elliot Smith, "Deutsche Bank shares slip amid $20 billion Russian money-laundering allegations," CNBC, April 18, 2019, https://www.cnbc.com/2019/04/18/deutsche-bank-shares-slip-amid-20-billion-russian-money-laundering-allegations.html.

Jodi Vittori, "How Anonymous Shell Companies Finance Insurgents, Criminals, and Dictators," Council on Foreign Relations, September 7, 2017. https://www.cfr.org/report/how-anonymous-shell-companies-finance-insurgents-criminals-and-dictators.

Amelia Wade, "Cryptocurrency Scams On the Rise," Which? March 29, 2018, https://www.which.co.uk/news/2018/03/cryptocurrency-scams-on-the-rise/.

Index